THE AUTHORITY CODE

HOW TO POSITION, MONETIZE, AND SELL YOUR EXPERTISE

ROCHELLE MOULTON

COVER DESIGN BY: XAVIER COMAS

LAYOUT DESIGN BY: OPEYEMI IKUBORIJE

FOR INFORMATION ABOUT SPECIAL DISCOUNTS FOR BULK PURCHASES, PLEASE VISIT _WWW. ROCHELLEMOULTON.COM_

ISBN: 979-8-9851089-0-3 (e-book)

ISBN: 979-8-9851089-1-0 (paperback)

ISBN: 979-8-9851089-2-7 (audio)

LIBRARY OF CONGRESS CONTROL NUMBER: 2021921035

Praise for *The Authority Code*

"There are millions of experts, but far, far fewer authorities. Rochelle Moulton knows the difference. More importantly, she can clearly explain the difference; most importantly, she offers a wealth of practical examples to show the reader the 'how' of doing it. If I had had this book back when, it would have saved me a decade in my own journey."

Charles H. Green, co-author of *The Trusted Advisor*

"If you struggle with how to sell your expertise, this book is for you. The Authority Code is packed with fresh insights, practical tools and rock-solid strategies that will change how you sell forever."

Jill Konrath, author of *More Sales, Less Time, Agile Selling, SNAP Selling, and Selling To BIG Companies*

"Being an expert without actually impacting your world is like wetting your pants in a dark suit: you get a warm feeling, but nobody is going to notice. Rochelle's blueprint for impact is designed to take that spark of authority and turn it into a roaring flame that will consume the obstacles that prevent true authorities from really making a difference."

David C. Baker, author of *The Business of Expertise*

"This book is a must-read for anyone who wants to be recognized for the skill, talent, and yes, genius, that they possess. The Authority Code gives you a framework and exercises that will help you reach, influence, and impact your market in ways that only true authorities can."

April Dunford, author of *Obviously Awesome*

"Taking a topic that is clouded in mystery and making it approachable, accessible and authentic is a tall order. Rochelle Moulton nails it—The Authority Code is a practical guide full of authentic stories and purposeful exercises for experts ready to step into (and conquer) the authority space."

Michael F. Kay, CFP®, author of *The Business of Life* and *The Feel Rich Project*

CONTENTS

DEDICATION

For Harvey

INTRODUCTION

Authority And Why It Matters

I was twenty-six when the entire trajectory of my career changed for good.

As a junior consultant at a global consulting firm, I was selected to become the local "expert" on a new law that completely upended how our clients would deal with a sticky issue.

I worked many late nights, poring over hundreds of pages of legalese. I traded insights with my counterparts in other offices across the country. Then, as my confidence grew, I became excited to get out of the weeds and start briefing actual clients.

Since the issue was heating up in the marketplace, the practice leader decided to host an in-office client briefing and asked me to present. It would be my first-ever stint at the podium, and I was both thrilled and nauseated. And then the acceptances started rolling in. Instead of the thirty or so attendees we'd typically garner, we quickly had over 120—which put us at maximum capacity.

The senior consultants went into panic mode at the idea of a hot client event being led by the greenest member of the team. While their attempt to have me replaced was overruled by the managing partner, the compromise was a last-minute practice session.

The afternoon before the big day, I took my slides into a small, dark room to rehearse before the office leadership team—who proceeded to spend the next five hours arguing among themselves, critiquing, changing, and (sometimes, viciously) tearing apart my deck.

When it was finally over, I was up until 2 a.m., revising, rehearsing, and mostly praying I wouldn't suck.

One hundred seven people showed up that day (yes, I counted), and we had a lively discussion about what the new law would mean for them. Could I have been better? No doubt. But I was prepared, and most of all, I was me.

That sometimes mean-spirited grilling session was, in hindsight, a pure gift because it taught me an early, valuable lesson: it wasn't about me; it was about the audience. It's about how you use your expertise to transform your audience.

For that, they gave the session rave reviews. Word spread, and it wasn't long before I was speaking outside the firm and snagging some national podium time. The visibility I earned led to my becoming president of an 800-member industry association, all before the ripe old age of thirty. This was topped like a cherry by a partnership in the firm at thirty-one.

It was the start of my authority journey. It gave me a front-row seat to the power of authority and how to use it to reach more of the people I most wanted to serve and build several vibrant, sustainable consulting businesses.

I became fascinated by the career arcs of the experts and authorities surrounding me. Between my experiences at that giant consulting firm (ten years including a partnership) and another six years cofounding and building a boutique advisory from scratch, I started to codify best practices in building true market authority.

But it wasn't until I sold my firm to Arthur Andersen that I genuinely understood the total value of building a name for yourself. They not only paid a premium for our reputation; we were able to add another zero to the price tag.

That got my attention.

Until then, I thought authority was only about building your expertise so clients would hire you. I missed the larger concept of value creation—and the power to reach, influence, and ultimately, impact your market segment in ways only authorities can.

Authority matters.

Because when you build suitable authority in your niche, you have your choice of how you want to play. At its best, work feels less like, well, work and more like a mission that you're excited to fulfill. Authority gives you choices.

So what is authority exactly? Almost every dictionary defines it as being an expert. But actual market authority is about much more than expertise. Experts command deep knowledge, but authorities also command influence.

There is a difference.

By the time I started working with Arthur Andersen tax partners, that difference was obvious. The experts—and the halls were littered with them—knew a great deal about their subject matter. They were often brilliant, provided you were willing to sift through some ponderous explanations on obscure topics.

But the authorities had a clear edge. They knew how to speak the language of their audience. I watched them translate their expertise into valuable nuggets, varying the delivery depending on their client. They had a habit of reaching inside themselves to make connections their peers did not. Of building rapport through empathy, even when it was from a large stage.

I realized that the authorities who were irresistibly spreading their ideas and profitably building their tribes followed a pattern.

After Andersen imploded (I spent the next five years coaching other consulting firm partners and leading a Fortune 500 consulting division), I kept seeing the same patterns for building successful market authority.

It got to the point where I could predict who would be most likely to succeed and who would not.

But it wasn't how you'd think.

It wasn't because some were smarter or more talented, worked harder, or had more money to play with. None of those factors made a difference. Instead, it boiled down to applying a repeatable series of decisions, habits, and actions, all of which can be learned, practiced, and mastered.

I call it "The Authority Code."

Since 2007, I've been test-driving this process to transform consultants and big thinkers into authorities, and it works. Now, I want to show you how to use this roadmap and way of thinking to create your own custom authority strategy and action plan. The goal?

To give you—an independent freelancer or consultant—the tools, the blueprint, the mindset, and the confidence to build a happy, profitable, six-figure-plus authority business faster than you would alone.

You deserve to reach your full potential as an authority, where you're doing what you love (think: working 100 percent in your genius zone) and being paid handsomely for it.

If you've ever been frustrated when you see an "expert" in your space spread their ideas and influence seemingly effortlessly while you struggle for traction, you know what I mean.

In this book, I will show you the specific steps and actions to build your own business and influence as an unforgettable authority.

I share twelve exercises (in this book and in a companion Workbook you can download at *www.rochellemoulton.com/workbook*. These will guide you to uncover your unique attributes and clarify your vision so that you can position (Chapters 1 through 5), monetize (Chapter 6), and sell (Chapters 7 through 9) your authority to your ideal audience.

My fondest wish is for you to approach this book and these exercises with a fresh perspective. This process will build your confidence, not only in your own brand of expertise, but in your ability to successfully—and happily—monetize it. After all, when it comes to selling authority, the first sale you make is to yourself.

Once you begin thinking of yourself as driving down the road to authority, your mindset starts to shift. It's no longer about working with any client that walks in your (virtual) door. Instead, it's about seeking out the right clients. About doing work that significantly transforms a group of people you care about. About building a body of work vs. a series of engagements.

Nine elements make up The Authority Code—each one gets its own chapter and exercise(s), so you can decide exactly how to apply each concept to your business. Let's take a quick look at what's coming.

Embrace The "V" Word

Your job as an authority is to embrace your vision, to design the world you want to live in—and figure out how to describe it in vivid detail—so your ideal clients and buyers want to live there too. It's like an outsized version of the fort you built as a kid, the one you designed so you and your BFFs could kick back and live the lives you imagined.

What's The Revolution You Want To Lead?

How will you change your world—what's the ultimate mission that drives your business? And I mean big: crazily, mightily, horror movie scaringly big. It's impossible to drill down into your unique brand as an authority until you get exquisitely clear on the transformation you're midwifing to your ideal audience.

Your Ideal Client: Who Energizes And Inspires You?

There's magic in choosing an audience that energizes and inspires you. You can't wait to learn more about their challenges and figure out how to solve their most vexing problems. The deeper you understand them, the more entrenched you—and your business—become until you are the only obvious choice.

Niche: Because You Don't Become A Hero By Being Like Everybody Else

Picking a niche allows you to develop white space; a corner of the market that you can own and have a rocking good time building out. Choosing the right niche, and staying enchanted with it, allows you to stay happily engrossed in your subject matter for years to come while growing expertise that you can sell at a premium.

Tell Your Story So It Doesn't Suck

We humans are hardwired to listen to—and learn from—stories. Sure, straight-up wisdom is powerful, but what your audience craves is a powerful origin story. Why do you care so much about the clients and buyers you're serving? Why have you committed to this niche and revolution?

Monetize Your Expertise

You can't create a sustainable and happy business until you effectively monetize your expertise. That means you'll need a system to build leverage and value inside your business that matches how you most want to work. Only then can you regularly take time away from the business to reflect and think big—and to carve out whatever defines a happy life for yourself.

Learn To Publish Like It's A Revenue Stream (Because It Is)

Publishing is one of the three sales tools of authority builders that is essential to break away from the freelancer trap of selling yourself as an extra pair of hands. Publishing—whether writing, podcasting, or creating videos—in the right lanes of content will position you to attract better clients at higher fees.

Enlist Your Authority Circle—Your Rat Pack, Apostles, And Tribal Leaders

Many so-called experts love to talk about thrashing the competition and "winning" all the marbles, like building your business is a zero-sum game. It isn't. Authorities thrive by figuring out who to cooperate with, spend time courting them, and collaborate for mutual benefit instead of worrying about who is winning.

Master The Gentle Art Of Persuasion So You'll Never Have To Sell Again

Buyers of expertise want to be gently persuaded by your point of view, your track record, and how you demonstrably care about them and their challenges. They don't want to be sold; in fact, your ideal clients will wind up selling YOU on working together when you've consistently demonstrated your value and fit.

The last chapter is how to **Take Your Authority Out For A Spin;** developing a workable action plan to propel you and your business into authority territory.

The trick to building an authority business well and with joy is developing and maintaining an authority mindset. Where leveraging your expertise becomes a constant drumbeat as you build your business, your career, and your reputation. Where you're serving your very best audience, the very best of you.

So get that picture firmly in your head as we get started. You're not only building a business, you're also developing a body of work—human interactions, thoughtful content, and positive influence—that you can be proud of.

Let's do this!

CHAPTER 1

EMBRACE THE "V" WORD

"You are not here merely to make a living. You are here in order to enable the world to live more amply, with greater vision, with a finer spirit of hope and achievement. You are here to enrich the world, and you impoverish yourself if you forget the errand." —**Woodrow Wilson**

When it comes to building a viable authority business—one with long-term sustainability—the first step is to decide where you're going.

When people tell me they want to start a business selling their expertise, I start asking questions to understand what they really want to build . . . and why. *What problems do you most want to solve? Who are you excited to help? What kind of business do you want to create?*

Whenever I hear, "I just want to get out of my job and have some freedom around the work I do—I don't want to limit myself," I know it's just a matter of time before they run out of clients. The storyline that you've left corporate and hung out your own shingle is good for a year or two, tops, as a client-attraction message. By then, if you haven't started marketing yourself from a well-honed specialist position, you're stuck.

You can't compete for work on a national (much less international) level because there's nothing especially remarkable about what you do, how you do it, or who you're doing it for.

The most you can hope for without authority is to become a local execution-style knowledge worker. Web design for small companies who drive you batty, writing marketing copy for a bunch of one-off campaigns, or selling yourself as an extra pair of hands to a firm that sells better than you (and marks you up 1-3X, pocketing the profit that could have been yours).

In any of those scenarios, the difference is control. Who has it, who uses it, and who makes money from it. So why not take the reins yourself?

The beauty is it's not hard to lead the show. But you have to start with a clear vision, the V-word, of where you want to take yourself, your ideas, and the people you plan to serve. Don't worry—you can change your mind as you get some experience under your belt (I'd be surprised if you didn't).

The important thing is to start visioning—and then to keep writing it down.

Decide Where You're Going

Let's begin with the end in mind, as Stephen Covey would have said. While ultimately, your emphasis will be on serving a specific slice of a paying marketplace—your target market—I want you to start with your end goal of building an authority business.

Think about that. What does success look like for you and your business? And before you answer that, I'm inviting you to open yourself up to what COULD be, rather than just accept what you think is possible. Because an earth-thumping vision is not about the status quo, it's about *feeling*. It's about *desire*. It's about wanting your dream enough to fight for it.

Why not direct all the grit, determination, and energy you'll pour into your business into something that truly matters to you? That allows you to enrich the world with your unique talents and passions? And that will enable you to live the life and lifestyle that suits you best?

Exactly.

Did Somebody Say Vision?

A lot of times when I ask a consultant about their vision, as in, "What's your vision for your business; not your client's business, but your own?", they stumble around and will say something like this:

> Well, when I started the business, I imagined I'd spend all my time serving fabulous clients at premium rates, but the reality is the opposite. I'm running on a hamster wheel trying to keep up—when I have enough work, I worry

about getting it done, and when I don't, I'm scurrying to get new clients.

Does that sound like a vision to you? No, not to me either—at least not one I'd get excited about.

One financial planner said something like this when I asked him the very same question:

> Every day, I help families improve their relationship with money. But what I've come to realize is that when you help one family change, it doesn't just help their immediate family. It transforms every single generation that comes after. I want to find a way to reach many more families that can't afford to hire me personally, so they and their children and their grandchildren can live happier, easier lives.

Don't you love that? The raw emotion—the power of his vision—comes through loud and clear. And it is this vision that drives him every single day as he grows his practice, hires other planners, and serves clients.

That's because the right vision will energize and inspire you and, over time, attract a tribe of the like-minded to you, your ideas, services, products, and business.

So that's where we're headed. But first, we're going to do some stage-setting.

You want to make sure that the business you're designing and building is EXACTLY what you want on a very personal level—which is especially important if you have even the mildest tendency to put others' needs before your own.

Before you turn another page, go to _www. rochellemoulton.com/workbook_ and download your free copy of the companion Workbook I developed so you can track your responses to all of the questions and exercises I pose in this book. There is also some bonus material to help you think through each exercise in more detail. Know that while you'll get great value from reading this book, your most profound value will come from applying the principles behind The Authority Code to your own situation.

EXERCISE 1: DEFINE YOUR VISION

Consider these four questions:

> What do you want for your life?

> What are your dreams?

> What do you want to create?

> What does living and working well look like?

Be gut-clenchingly specific. You are designing your life and your business, and you get to decide what is gonna float your boat and inspire your dedication. What are the dreams that you've only dared to flirt with, and perhaps have never even spoken out loud?

As you position your business for success on _your_ terms, this is the time to get everything down. Soak on it and decide what gets pride of place in your vision.

I've been asking these same questions for almost fifteen years in my work with private clients. And I've found there is always a surprise (or two) that comes out of this exercise.

Even when my clients felt clear about what they wanted to accomplish, something just below the surface came out with a bit of prodding. And it was only rarely about making more money (that was usually already on their list). Their real desire? More time and the freedom to spend it the way they want. Like:

> I want to spend two to three months every year on a health care mission to Africa.

> We want to start a family, and I want to cut back my schedule to be a majorly active dad.

> I'm ready to invest in creating passive income streams; my family wants to move to a small town in Europe so we can spend the next few years immersed in a new culture.

> I want to keep singing in a traveling choir—my passion— so I need to serve clients remotely as much as possible.

> I want to buy a hobby farm where I'll have more room to foster kids who need a family.

> I am appalled at how few women there are in the upper echelons of tech and want to use my skills to get more into positions of influence and power.

You get the gist.

Your vision is about the fundamental way you want to shift the world. It might start small, within your immediate grasp, like earning enough to pay the rent. And hey, that's an essential first hurdle in your business.

But to power a long-term sustainable business, we need to think bigger than ourselves. It's about the problems you solve and the people you serve. It's the story you tell them about where you're going together.

When I cofounded my first firm, we had a bright and shining vision that mattered deeply: building a close-knit band of "refugees" from the big firms who wanted to do great work, minus the eighty-hour weeks and living out of a suitcase. We believed that our model would produce better outcomes for our clients and better lives for all of us.

It was no big surprise that we had a deep pool of highly talented consultants (women, especially) who wanted to work with us. But the vision appealed every bit as much to our mostly Fortune 500 clients—it turned out to be highly sticky since they were grappling with many of the same issues in attracting and keeping top talent. That stickiness produced referrals and introductions that were not only unusual in the insular world of Fortune 500 consulting, but accounted for many of our early wins.

We also got a lot of (free) buzz, including being featured in a *Wall Street Journal* cover story about small firms making big waves in new work arrangements. And eventually, as I mentioned earlier, we attracted Arthur Andersen, who was happy to pay a hefty premium for the reputation we built as we kept executing our vision.

Having a vision that binds your people to you is a powerful thing—it serves as a catalyst, growing your connections and influence exponentially when you start living it out loud.

Now that you've figured out what YOU need to feel happy and successful in your business, you can turn to how you're going to serve your ideal clients and buyers. Again, it boils down to the purpose behind what you're doing.

EXERCISE 2: THE CORE PURPOSE OF YOUR AUTHORITY

Adam Leipzig (the film and theatre producer/writer) does a brilliant job talking about life purpose in his TEDx talk, "How To Know Your Life Purpose in 5 Minutes." I've adapted his questions here to apply to how you think about the purpose of your authority:

> What I love to do most in the world is . . .
>
> The one thing I feel supremely qualified to teach others is . . .
>
> Who am I doing this for? Whom do I most want to teach and reach? (Imagine you only work with your favorite kinds of people. Who are they? What do they have in common?)
>
> The people I serve want or need . . .
>
> How the people I serve transform after they've experienced me . . .

Note the emphasis on service?

Because the core purpose of your authority is not about you—it's about how you USE YOUR GIFTS TO SERVE OTHERS. Getting clear on how this ties into your vision of life and business will help guide you to become a generous and trusted authority.

Make no mistake, the kind of market authority we're talking about here is deeply rooted in generosity. Think about the experts in your space that you tune into regularly. Are they hoarding information? Or sharing as they learn?

When they're selling to you, are they loading up on hype, trying to pull everyone into their offers—or are they carefully targeting those who would benefit most? Authentic authority is generous; we don't want you buying things that won't get you results.

One well-known "authority" displays a veneer of generosity; he gives a few things away to his readers and has written some beneficial books. The problem? He adopts a surly and often elitist demeanor on social media that is the opposite of generous—and while he attracts a core following, his public persona will always put a ceiling on his success.

When you're the brain surgeon saving clients from the brink of death, you can sometimes get away with being a jerk. But authorities relying on the generosity of others to spread their wisdom? Not so much. Generosity is not only the wiser path; it's a heck of a lot more fun.

Tapping Into Your Genius Zone

The word *genius* comes from ancient Rome, where they believed an inner spirit watches over each of us, guiding us to our calling. Your genius arises from the deepest part of you; ignore it at your peril.

That voice telling you that your introverted self didn't fit in a firm of howling extroverts? That was your genius telling you *Get out now.*

Here's the thing. You—like every human on this planet—have a genius zone. It's that work where you fall into flow, where you lose track of time as you tap into your unique talents and passions.

The single best thing you can do to build a happy and successful authority business is to figure out your genius zone and spend as much of your working time as possible there.

Think about that for a moment. If you're happiest teaching a room full of real estate agents how to sell, wouldn't you outsource everything else you possibly could? Sure, you'd spend some solo time preparing for your sessions, but you wouldn't be doing your taxes or coding your website. Instead, you'd 100 percent focus on doing what you're best at so you can deliver your genius to your ideal people as often as possible.

Or, said another way, every moment you spend on something someone else can do better, is a moment you're cheating the world of your talents.

Rather puts a different spin on this, doesn't it? Not only are you helping yourself by positioning your work smack dab in your genius zone, but you're making the world a much better place.

Besides deciding to spend the vast majority of your day doing exactly the work you adore, chances are, this is also your highest value work—where you can charge a premium price and work with your favorite type of clients.

Don't fall into the trap of undervaluing what comes naturally to you. Just because you can quickly capture the merits of a beauty product and tell its story to captivate customers doesn't mean your clients can. And while we'll talk more about specializing and niching in Chapter 4, rest assured that when you match up your genius zone with the folks you most want to serve, you'll be charging at the premium end of the spectrum.

We're talking about the kind of work where sometimes you just scratch your head, wondering how you got to be so lucky.

EXERCISE 3: PINPOINT YOUR GENIUS ZONE

1. What lights you up? Quick, name five things you love to do. Don't stop to think, just write.

2. Now, spend a little time considering your talents and your passions, the ones you can't live without. Seriously, you feel like you'd die if you couldn't do them. Write them all down here. (Tip: Struggling with some talents that just don't light you up anymore? It may be high time to kick those to the curb.)

3. Think about a time when you felt at the very top of your game—slam-dunking good. What were you doing? Who were you doing it with? Where were you?

4. What have you created when you felt most open, when love for what you were doing coursed through your veins? Who did you create it for and with?

5. What kinds of problems do you solve? What do people ask you for over and over again?

6. What do you love to do so much you might even do it without pay?

7. How do you make people feel? What does your audience (clients, colleagues, associates, readers, members) take away from their experience with you?

8. What do you do that changes the lives of those around you, even for a moment?

Now, look back on all your responses and thoughtfully answer these questions:

9. The five to ten things I'm incredibly good at AND love to do are:

10. The people who need and want my talents—the ones I resonate with on the highest level—are:

11. I make my best audiences feel:

Now put all of those together in a statement or two outlining the critical elements of your genius zone.

Example 1: I like working with hard-charging entrepreneurs— usually the CEO—who know what they want and make decisions fast. I prefer to focus on privately held tech companies that are well past the seed stage.

Example 2: I work best with VPs running operations in banking and financial services. Growing their operation should be one of their top three priorities. They should believe that they can't win without a strong team and are willing to invest time and money in building theirs.

Example 3: My time is best spent with women business owners in the retail space who want to grow beyond a single store and integrate bricks and mortar with their web storefront. They like to work collaboratively and aren't afraid to try new ideas—or shelve those that aren't working.

Don't worry, we'll flesh out more of your positioning in the coming chapters.

For now, it's enough that you know the conditions you need to perform your highest best work.

The last bit of advice on any talents that you're just not feeling anymore: This is the perfect time to drop them from your repertoire. When running your own business, why would you want to drag over talents you're no longer interested in using?

I once was very proud of my ability to walk into a firm of warring partners—the kind who couldn't agree on whether the sun was shining—and get them to consensus (it's a leftover skill from my days making big mergers work). Then, one day, dealing with a particularly difficult situation, it occurred to me that I didn't need to do this anymore. Just because I *could* do it didn't mean I *had* to do it.

Instead, now I use that particular skill to coach clients through difficult interpersonal situations. It's way more fun, still uses a piece of my genius zone, and I feel I'm using my talents for good instead of enabling bad behavior.

It's a great reminder of why we're discussing your vision here in this first chapter: This is your chance to create EXACTLY the life and business you want for yourself and those you love.

Every single line of your vision should sing to you and make you deliriously happy just thinking about it.

Takeaways on embracing the "V" word:

- To power a long-term sustainable business, we need to think bigger than ourselves.

- Crafting your vision means harnessing all the grit, determination, and energy you'll pour into your business into something that truly matters to you.

- Designing your vision is about control over your future: Who has it, who uses it, and who makes money from it.

- Get exquisitely clear on where you're going with your business: *What problems do you most want to solve? Who are you excited to help? What kind of business do you want to create?*

- Think beyond just making more money (of course you want that)—what's your genuine desire and purpose with your business?

- Your best vision for yourself will tap into your genius zone—where you fall into a flow and operate on all cylinders.

- Develop the mindset that you're serving the world best when you spend as much time as possible working in your genius zone.

- Serve your slice of the market. What about your vision is exciting and compelling to *your* people?

CHAPTER 2

WHAT'S THE REVOLUTION
YOU WANT TO LEAD?

"Now and then, someone is able to look at an empty space, conclude it would be a great place to start a revolution, and bravely go forward." —Henry Rollins

Does the thought of leading a revolution send shivers down your spine?

Good; that's an excellent place to start. Because leading a revolution—even a small one—requires humility along with a little healthy ego. You'll need the ego for the courage to put your ideas out there for challenging, but humility will guide you to listen and engage with the tribe you start enlisting.

But let's address the logical question first: Why start a revolution at all? Why not just quietly serve clients and steadily build a six-figure authority business?

Sure, you can 100 percent skip this whole revolution thing (just don't be tempted to avoid this because you're an introvert—more on that later). But your business growth will come agonizingly slowly because it's too hard for your audience to figure out what you stand for. Why do you exist? Why should they hire you vs. the other guy—and there's always another guy—who charges less?

Or, you could build a tidy little freelance business hiring yourself out by the hour, especially if your skill is in high demand, like software development or ad copywriting.

But ultimately, you'll hit one of two inflection points: not enough clients (which is bad enough) or such a steady demand that you create your very own hamster wheel, locked into income limited by the hours you can work. And eventually, if you don't burn out, you'll get bored.

That's when a revolution starts to sound enticing.

Designing The Revolution You Want To Lead

So what *exactly* is a revolution when it comes to your expertise and building your business?

Ask yourself: How do I want to transform my corner of the world with my work?

This goes beyond what consumer brand managers call the big idea—what your cheese, booze, or car is promising to contribute to your life.

To build lasting market authority as a soloist or leader of a boutique firm, you need more than a slogan; you must lead a movement. And it's far better to be bold than safe. Because when you anchor your work as part of a bigger, strategic outcome your client cares deeply about, pretty much everything you do gets easier.

You differentiate your services from all the other tactical choices your competitors are pushing.

You spark deeper conversations with your prospects, which means you wind up offering more transformational choices (that may well add an extra zero to your fees).

You find your services are value priceable, enabling you to not only deliver more significant outcomes but charge accordingly.

Let me be clear: There's nothing wrong with offering tactical services your client needs. It's a time-honored way to grow an advice business. But when you anchor those tactics into a larger strategic frame, you create growth opportunities for both you and your client.

THAT'S the territory of authority.

Like Charles H. Green, whose book *The Trusted Advisor* is still performing high in its Amazon category, *twenty years later.* His revolution coalesced around the idea that trust matters. He and his team burrowed deep into the market space where people in organizations have to persuade others—think sales and advisory work.

Their precise niche positioning in one-to-one trust in business advisory has led to developing multiple services, assessments (you can take their Trust Quotient Assessment on their website), and licensed global partners, all spreading the same message. And funding the revolution they believe in.

Nothing is off limits for your revolution if you feel it strongly enough to go all in. Jennifer Armbrust founded Sister, where her mission is to bring feminist business principles into business practices. She's created a twelve-principle framework for prototyping a feminist business (manifestos are a clarion call to get your peeps to join your revolution), along with a business model that's heavy on courses and teaching.

And even a small team can take corporate America by storm. Liz Wiseman, author of *Multipliers: How The Best Leaders Make Everyone Smarter,* used her book to spark a conversation way back in 2010 ("What if you could double your team's intelligence?") that continues today. It not only gave her firm a powerful message but a mega pulpit to deliver it from.

The beauty of creating your own revolution is that there are no boundaries to what is possible. You can serve large corporate audiences like Charles Green and Liz Wiseman or small independents like Jennifer Armbrust and moi. The world is your oyster.

When I first started my current business, I wasn't sure exactly what I wanted to do, I just knew that I'd had quite enough of big firms attempting to snuff the life out of me.

So I started by meeting with people I knew to see what kinds of problems I might solve. Finally, after a dozen or so of these, I had my "aha" moment that sparked my next chapter.

I had two back-to-back meetings with strategy consultants. Both were soloists, top drawer brilliant with virtually identical websites and marketing collateral. The problem? Their work and their styles could not have been more different. How were their ideal clients supposed to find them?

Plus, their messaging was stuck in typical big-firm consulting-ease: "We're smart, and we solve complex problems for anyone." Not surprisingly, both were desperate for leads and clients.

Once I saw the problem, I was hooked. After more research confirming this was widespread and causing unnecessary pain and suffering (and that no one else had targeted this market), I realized I'd found my niche.

So, I spent the next six months developing and testing my process with a beta group of solo consultants. I tweaked it and then officially launched my business with an inside-out form of authority branding based on their personal experiences, talents, and passions tied to a white-space market segment.

White space—an unclaimed market territory that you can own—was like the magic key that turned the lock. It's positioning yourself in precisely the right space so that you're uniquely memorable.

So I started using "Be unforgettable" as my call to revolution. I attempted to name the deep desire we all have to be seen and valued for our true selves and contributions. It's not about being a celebrity but about putting your talents in service to whatever greater good speaks to your soul.

EXERCISE 4: DESIGN YOUR REVOLUTION

Go back to your answers to EXERCISE 3: PINPOINT YOUR GENIUS ZONE in Chapter 1. I want you to copy your genius zone statement so it's front and center, e.g., I like working with hard-charging entrepreneurs—usually the CEO—who know what they want and make decisions fast. I prefer to focus on privately held tech companies that are well past the seed stage.

Then, bring over your answers to these questions from EXERCISE 1: DEFINE YOUR VISION

> What kinds of problems do you solve?
>
> What do people ask you for over and over again?
>
> What do you do that changes the lives of those around you, even for a moment?

Those are the first breadcrumbs that will point to the right revolution for you to lead. As you look those over, start digging a little deeper:

> What is frustrating about your field that, if reconfigured, would add joy, purpose, and/or a significant bottom-line impact to your peers and clients?
>
> What big problems do you see as solvable that everyone else believes are impossible to fix?
>
> How might you—working from your genius zone—transform the current state of your favorite people?

If you're having trouble getting clear on this, it might be worth calling in some reinforcements. Pick your all-time favorite clients, buyers, readers (five to eight will probably give you enough data points) and ask three pointed questions:

- What is irresistible about working with me?

- What experience (feeling) do you get from me that you don't get from anyone else?

- What do you consistently rely on me for?

Make a list of what you hear from them. Circle anything you hear more than once. Put a star by anything you hear three or more times. Hint: Your special sauce is in the stars.

Once you are clear about your unique value, passions, and motivation (this is not the time for modesty), you are ready to put it all together into a statement that captures it. Ready?

Complete this statement:

I_____ (insert action verb) _____ (insert your best audience) _____ (insert how you make your best audience feel or an outcome they can consistently rely upon).

A few examples to stoke your creativity:

I build wealth for risk-takers.

I teach lawyers to sell more business.

I create beloved companies.

I guide business owners to feel rich no matter how much money they have.

I make consultants and big thinkers unforgettable.

Take some time with this. Leave it and come back to it. Ruminate. Salivate. It should scare you a little—as in "Who am I to think this big?"

Your final step is to turn your statement into a big, bold idea that irresistibly draws your best audience to you. Use as few words as possible while still making it rich and compelling. Focus on the intersection of what makes your heart beat faster with where your best talents lie. Those examples above morphed themselves into these big ideas:

> Never follow.

> Make it rain.

> Become a beloved company.

> Feel rich.

> Be unforgettable.

Get the idea? Now it's your turn. My big idea for the revolution I want to lead is:

Here's the thing about revolutions: they're never perfect. They require a particular sort of mindset; you've got to be willing to get messy with your ideas. To listen to and act on critical feedback from your audience. To even change course sometimes. Just like no plan survives the first encounter with the enemy, no successful revolution looks the same once you start sharing it.

The Passion Economy Revolution

Take Adam Davidson, award-winning journalist, cofounder, and former cohost of NPR's "Planet Money," who wrote the best-selling *The Passion Economy: The New Rules for Thriving in the Twenty-First Century.* His revolution? That to ultimately succeed in our careers, we must embrace our unique passions.

And not in a follow-your-bliss sort of way, but with discipline and rigor, which is one of the reasons I find talking with Adam so fascinating. "The *passion* word really should convey 'I'm going to put me and the wholeness of me into the way I make a living.' It's a strong choice. It's not a trivial choice. It possibly isn't for everyone."

Publishing the book wasn't just his stake in the ground for The Passion Economy revolution but also became the catalyst for a fundamental change in how he runs his business. As he puts it:

> When you work in the gatekeeper economy (like say, for a magazine), you don't know the unique value you're creating. There may be added prestige and reputation, but you're part of a bundled product and your success is tied to theirs. When you work in the direct-to-consumer economy, you're super aware of your buyer and exactly how you deliver value. I don't ever again want a single person to determine my success.

Writing his first book forced him to operate differently. Rather than staying in journalist mode, which often requires some very generalist thinking, he went narrow, continually refining and tightening his ideas. Birthing the book felt like he was saying "Here is my thing" in a way he hadn't done before. He planted his flag.

Now that he's leading a revolution instead of being a pure journalist, he gets very different feedback from his audience. Instead of a cocktail party conversation on his latest article, now he hears about how he's changed lives. And as we all know, helping people is why we do this work and what feels so good. Today, Adam's number one business priority is to dig deeper into his audience. To understand them inside and out so that he can figure out how to help them and bring "genuine joy." He is 100 percent audience-focused (leading a revolution will do that for you).

His business and revenue model has also done a 180. Instead of most income coming from gatekeepers, his solo enterprise now has multiple revenue streams (we'll talk more about how to do that in Chapter 6) with no major reliance on any one of them. He maintains a writing contract with *The New Yorker*, juggles multiple movie and TV projects, does some consulting and speaking, and—in a hard nod to his revolution—created a new digital course around The Passion Economy. He's only one round into it, but all signs point to this being a significant revenue stream in his model for the future.

One more thoughtful outcome of this particular revolution: Adam's barometer in deciding how to move forward with new projects. He measures them on four scales: fun, money, glory (for the project), and passion—and uses the scale to decide whether and when to make trade-offs. For example, if a new opportunity is all about the mission, the money isn't so important. But if a project isn't fun, on mission, or creating glory for the team, it had better pay REALLY well to earn a yes.

Starting Your Revolution

The best revolutions, where you're genuinely Passion Economy passionate, can be damned scary to begin. If you want to make an impact, you've got to honestly and viscerally believe you can make a dent in the problem you're tackling. Yes, you'll feel fear—who doesn't? But you'll push through it if you believe in your cause enough to fight for it.

Like my client Rebecca, who became a social marketing expert in the global drowning community (yes, that's a thing). She started slowly learning the field and connecting with recognized experts to understand the problems and current solutions. She became convinced there was not enough attention paid to children drowning. Did you know that after congenital disabilities, drowning kills more one-to-four-year-old children than anything else?

As a mother, she felt this was unacceptable and quickly decided to focus her attention on saving kids from drowning. But it was far from an easy choice.

She wasn't always readily accepted in the established water safety community—who was she to be thinking so big? Coming from a non-academic background, she constantly dealt with voices of the establishment trying to keep her off the critical industry podiums.

Thinking about herself as the leader of a revolution helped her stay the course. It helped her identify and enlist the like-minded to keep pushing for new ideas (and funding). Of course, it wasn't easy or comfortable—but then, big change never is.

Today, she is the proud founder of a nonprofit with a deep global network and has developed widely used education and awareness strategies. She's coauthored a children's book (and is working on one for adults), spoken at conferences worldwide, and been named to several influential committees charged with drowning safety.

Instead of introducing herself as a social marketing expert—a bland statement without any punch—she proudly declares, "I save kids from drowning."

When you lead from your revolution, you hold yourself accountable to your vision and invite others to hold you accountable too. There is no place to hide.

If you want to sell your authority so you can build an endless pool of your ideal clients and buyers, you've got to stake your claim on a piece of white-space territory. The more aggressive your claim (while still being credible), the more attention it gets.

Keep sharpening the edges of your idea before you go public—you can even experiment in low-risk situations, like, say, a cocktail party. Rebecca's positioning and call to action evolved as a series of potential ideas (we explored these plus a few others before settling on the last):

Reduce global drowning deaths.

Save lives during natural disasters.

Save lives during floods.

Prevent backyard pool drownings.

Prevent drunk swimming accidents.

Prevent drowning while boating/sailing.

Save kids from drowning.

See how any one of these ideas could be a worthy starting point for a revolution? It just depends on what speaks to you—your talents, passions, and who you want to serve—and where there is a viable market for solutions.

Let's talk for a sec about what will make your revolution viable and bring some discipline and rigor to this process. Of course, completing the worksheets and drilling down to what really matters to you is crucial, but it's only half the challenge. You've also got to do a little research to ensure you're genuinely claiming white space.

Google is your friend here. Don't just check out a page or two of search results on your keywords. Instead, dig through the first ten. Is anyone using language similar to yours? That can be a sign you're on the right track—that there is an existing market for your revolution. But it's also a flashing yellow warning light to make sure you're not looking like a cheap imitation of someone who has already carved out the space you're eyeing.

Check out those in the spaces adjacent to yours (they may well become part of your Authority Circle that we'll discuss in Chapter 8). Might you collaborate with them in the future? Are your potential audiences similar enough that they might value knowing you both?

Once you're pretty confident you've identified your revolution, it's worth testing it on a few of your ideal people (we'll talk more about who those are in the next chapter). Here are the kinds of immediate emotional reactions that tell you you're on to something:

They immediately suggest people for you to talk to.

They latch on to a key phrase or two and don't let it go (people who haven't talked to me for a few years will still open new conversations with how they want to be unforgettable).

They tell you a story about how they faced the central issue in your revolution and either solved it or are still battling it.

They ask you to get in front of *their* audience: a guest post, a podcast interview, maybe a joint livestream.

They ask for help with their situation right now.

If you're not getting much traction with the idea with your ideal clients, you still have some work to do. It might be as simple as refining your messaging or tweaking your definition of an ideal client.

When I worked with "Twyla," she was unequivocal on her audience: training and development consulting firms. She knew their problems inside and out, having worked as a PR person at several of them. Unfortunately, her original idea of leveraging PR to spread their messages landed with a dull thud.

So I encouraged her to keep talking to their founders and heads of marketing, asking questions, and listening intently. It turns out they weren't interested in PR for PR's sake. Instead, they were looking for higher profile thought leadership for both their firms and a handful of their practice leaders. Her business and her entire experience changed when she looked beyond herself as simply a classic PR resource.

Once she partnered with her ideal audience, Twyla was able to craft not only a viscerally compelling revolution around building thought leadership in that space, but a six-figure retainer business. Her new vision gave her a platform to build, clear allies to align with, and an ongoing influential role in her industry.

One final thing about revolutions: No one leads them alone.

Of course, when you begin thinking about yours, you may well be solo. You're deciding where to stake the next chunk of your business life, and it has to make sense—to you. Just know that as you develop your idea and morph it into a revolution (lots more about this in Chapter 8, I promise), your job is to find ways to bring the like-minded into your fold.

Thinking about who else in related universes you might align with is part of the excitement. You get to consider not only what revolution you'll lead but who you want to hold up the banners with you as you march.

Takeaways on leading your revolution:

- By choosing to lead a revolution, you give yourself many more pathways to quickly build a viable, sustainable, and happy authority business.

- Leading a revolution is your opportunity to claim "white space"—a market segment that no one else is occupying.

- Your first decision: How do you want to transform your corner of the world with your work?

- Your second decision: Who do you want to come with you?

- The only boundaries to starting a revolution are those you decide to place yourself.

- Soloists are leading some of the most intriguing and successful revolutions; size is not a barrier.

- When you viscerally believe you can make a dent in the problem you're tackling, you'll start making an impact the second you begin.

- Developing the mindset of leading a revolution is the beginning of building true authority.

CHAPTER 3

YOUR IDEAL CLIENT: WHO ENERGIZES AND INSPIRES YOU?

"Our chief want is someone who will inspire us to be what we know we could be." —*Ralph Waldo Emerson*

When you start your expertise business, it seems perfectly logical to grow your client base by looking to those with deep enough pockets to hire you, especially if you're starting a freelance business hiring yourself out by the hour or day. So why waste time talking to people who can't afford you?

But after the first year or two in business, you've probably run through all of the low-hanging fruit clients, i.e., people you don't have to sell (much) on hiring you. They liked your story of leaving corporate life—no more working for da man—and wanted to help pave an accessible runway for you to go solo.

31

If you have a highly in-demand skill, you might be able just to keep happily freelancing, practicing your craft until it turns into the hamster wheel that makes you crazy enough to rethink your business model. Or, you might be the one with that deer-in-the-headlights face when you realize you're going to have to start *selling* if you want to keep making money.

It's not surprising that Year 2 seems to be the demarcation line—you either figure out who you're going to serve (and how), or you make a hasty pivot back to being an employee.

There's a trick to embracing that stage of your business—and any stage where the work just isn't making you happy: Get exquisitely clear on your ideal client.

It's not about how much money is in their pockets—it's about who energizes and inspires you to serve them.

Don't worry, I'll show you how to monetize almost any audience provided you are curious about their problems, dreams, the reality of their situations, AND that you care enough about them to invest your time and energy in helping them get what they want.

So embrace the magic of choosing an audience that energizes and inspires you. Instead of dragging yourself to "work," you're humming to yourself, thinking about how lucky you are to be serving your client base. And in turn, your ideal clients and buyers feel that love (yes, I said *love*) and seek you out, happy to pay your premium prices.

Let's now focus just on discovering your people. Rest assured, we'll talk about how to specialize and carve out a market niche for yourself in the next chapter.

If you're already serving clients and simply want to zero in on your ideal sweet spot, skip ahead to the YOUR CLIENT AVATAR exercise. If you're not even sure where to begin, stay with me here for a little longer.

As a good starting point, look back to your answers to Question 3 in the PINPOINT YOUR GENIUS ZONE exercise: Think about a time when you felt at the very top of your game—slam-dunking good. What were you doing? Who were you doing it with? Where were you?

Focus on the "who"—who are your favorite people to work with? Working with your ideal people might feel like an unattainable luxury at first, but bear with me. When you worked a traditional job, you didn't have many choices about your colleagues or your boss—they were a package deal. But now, YOU get to decide who you'll be spending time with. Isn't it worth investing a little thought into what will make you happy?

"Stan" left a corporate gig because he couldn't take the toxic internal politics and wanted more freedom to decide who he'd work with. His first few clients were referrals from people he'd known from his old life—and while they were OK, he wasn't feeling energized or inspired by them or the work. But then he met his newest client, and it was as if the sun suddenly came out and the grass was greener, the air fresher. Everything felt different.

So we dialed in to what was so special about this new client and new assignment:

> The client had a massive goal—one that was daring, maybe even audacious—and that in no way was guaranteed.

The leader values the human side of the business and her team. And while she had plenty of formal education, she got where she is through hard work, smarts, and determination.

The client team was highly functional; they respected the leader and each other and collaboratively participated in their initial sales conversation.

Once the work began, they answered Stan's questions and readily shared information that he'd often had to beg for from other clients.

He felt he could speak directly to any team member, even when the inevitable challenges and differences of opinion arose. There was a culture of mutual respect and collaboration that made Stan feel like a valued advisor.

The leader was a good problem solver and was flexible when Stan suggested workarounds to save time, money, and sanity.

So let's unpack that for a moment. Just by looking at one great engagement, you can start to see what you value most (the reverse works for the stick-needles-in-my-eye projects too). And if you haven't had a stellar client yet, look back to your previous life. Think about the unique projects you worked on in your old job(s) and why you liked them so much.

What about the people, goal, project, role, timing, and outcome inspired you to work at your best? Of course, we all have different needs, which means there are no wrong answers here. The important thing is to discover who brings out the best in you— who inspires and energizes you to serve them?

You might find it helpful to drill down into the qualities or values of your favorite people to work with. Here is a word salad to help you choose the qualities that speak to you:

Accuracy, achievement, adventure, ambition, balance, beauty, belonging, calm, candor, caring, challenge, charm, clarity, cleanliness, comfort, compassion, competition, concentration, confidence, conformity, connection, consistency, control, cooperation, courage, courtesy, creativity, curiosity, daring, decisive, decorum, delight, dependability, determination, devotion, dignity, diligence, directness, discipline, discovery, diversity, dominance, drive, duty, dynamism, education, efficiency, elegance, empathy, energy, enthusiasm, excellence, expertise, fairness, faith, fame, family, fashion, fitness, flexibility, focus, freedom, fun, generosity, global, growth, happiness, harmony, health, honor, humility, humor, imagination, independence, ingenuity, insight, inspiration, integrity, intelligence, intensity, joy, justice, kindness, knowledge, leadership, learning, liberty, logic, love, loyalty, making a difference, mastery, maturity, motivation, neatness, optimism, order, originality, passion, peace, perseverance, philanthropy, play, pleasure, poise, polish, power, practical, precision, presence, professional, prosperity, prudence, punctuality, purity, realism, recognition, reliability, resilience, resolve, respect, rigor, sacrifice, satisfaction, security, sensitivity, serenity, service, sharing, significance, simplicity, sincerity, solitude, speed, spirit, spontaneity, stability, stealth, strength, structure, success, supremacy, surprise, synergy, teamwork, thoroughness, tradition, tranquility, trust, understanding, variety, vigor, vitality, warmth, wealth, winning, wisdom, wonder, zeal.

And if you don't see your ideal words—add them in! Because once you get this picture firmly in your mind, you're ready to describe your ideal client avatar.

EXERCISE 5: YOUR CLIENT AVATAR

You have an ideal client. They are real people with hopes, dreams, pains, and fears. Your job is to understand what motivates them so you can speak directly to them, connect with them, and engage with them.

I want you to sit back, close your eyes, and envision your ideal client or buyer. Give them a name. Note a few salient points about them—their age, their position, and any demographics that might be relevant.

> Example: Shawn is a forty-five-year-old Silicon Valley CEO/founder of a successful B2B SaaS business. He does well—but he has a bigger dream.

See what I mean? Capture the core motivation of your client. (Note: If you're having trouble choosing an avatar, envision your most incredible—actual or imagined—dream client.)

And then carefully consider some questions about them:

- What's their biggest source of pain? What do they wrestle with regularly?

- What's the tape that plays in their head at 2 a.m. when they can't sleep?

- What are their biggest fears?

- What's the biggest danger they see? And what's the biggest danger they can't see yet?

- What are their greatest opportunities?

- What are their fondest hopes and dreams?

- How do they transform after they work with you or buy your books, programs, and products? What do they become? How does their future life change as a result of your work?

In the Workbook, you'll find space to flesh out your client avatar(s), so you can describe them in vivid detail.

There is no shortcut to this step because until you know for sure the client you want to attract, it's pretty much impossible to fill your pipeline consistently and reliably with ideal clients and buyers.

Speaking To Your Ideal Clients

One client, let's call her Robin, was frustrated because she kept attracting what she called "broke and tortured" entrepreneurs.

She'd listen to their tale of woe, ask some insightful questions, and deliver a proposal outlining how she'd get them to the desired outcome. And then . . . crickets. When she'd follow up, she'd hear twenty-seven variations of "I'd really like to hire you—you are fabulous—but I am just so broke." Or, "I'm just too frazzled with everything else going on to do this with you right now." It was driving her crazy. And it wasn't helping her bottom line either.

We started by looking at her ideal clients from the Client Avatar exercise: busy entrepreneurs (she later narrowed them down to those building integrative health care ventures) who understood the value of strategic marketing and PR to grow their business.

But when we looked at her website copy, we found she hadn't tailored it to those strong entrepreneurial business people she adored helping. Instead, she used phrases like "you're overwhelmed" and "you're scared by . . ." Who do you suppose is attracted to that kind of language? Exactly: The broke and tortured who were beating a path to her door.

She also used power words like "fix," and "streamline," and "rebuild," which typically attract people who want significant changes. If this is your perfect client, those are excellent words; if not, use "fix" words very carefully. Usually, those who want big fixes come from a messy place, and you'll likely find a few "tortured" among them.

Robin's situation turned out to be an easy fix. We cleaned up the language on her site and she permanently removed a few words from her sales conversations. The next four opportunities that came to her (including one to speak to an integrative health audience) closed quickly at her highest prices.

The moral of the story: The voice you use—in person and in any marketing collateral or interviews—needs to speak to your ideal client.

The other lesson buried in Robin's situation is that we teach people how to treat us. When we speak to our audience as though they are in dire straits, we send them the message that we're happy to hold their hands through excruciating change. Perfect if that's your gig, but deadly if it isn't.

One final thought on Robin's case. Had she decided that the "broke and tortured" were actually her people (many a business model has built success on this), we would have figured out how best to monetize her services with that demo. And it probably wouldn't look anything like the high, one-to-one fee-for-service model that was causing her so much angst.

Pruning Your Client List

Once you've identified your ideal clients, should you prune your list?

In a word: Yes. After you go through this exercise, it's hard to unsee your bad-fit clients. That doesn't mean they're bad people or that your standards are too high—it means that when you let the bad fits go, you both can prosper at a higher level.

Think about that for a moment. Once you decide who you serve at your highest and best level (you're jamming on all cylinders in your genius zone producing stellar transformations), why would you want to work with anyone else?

Consciously or not, you're giving less of your talents to your bad-fit clients. I'd argue you're underserving them, and it's best for both parties to move on. My former virtual assistant was positively brilliant at this. Every so often, she'd casually drop into a conversation that she'd fired six or seven clients the week before.

Once in a while, there was a precipitating conflict, but more often, she just decided that she couldn't continue serving them from her genius zone. When we parted company after nine terrific years together, it was clear that we weren't ideal for each other any longer. Our goodbye was graceful and amicable.

Letting a bad-fit client go is a service to both parties. And the seemingly odd thing is that I've yet to hear a consultant complain after the deed was done. I think that's because we believe the problem must be with us as professional service providers; that we must twist ourselves like a pretzel to serve every member of our client base the way they demand.

Permitting ourselves to kiss our non-ideal clients goodbye feels like lifting a lead weight off our shoulders. As *The Business of Authority* podcast listener Mike R. wrote:

> I just fired my first client! . . . I terminated the engagement for nonperformance on the client's part. They simply were not doing what they signed up to do in terms of execution, and the engagement was no longer financially viable for me. What I got out of the engagement are roughly 529 red flags to look for and recognize. Quite frankly, I should have walked away sooner.

If you're less than thrilled with your client base, one place to start is by force-ranking your clients from best to worst (you probably already know who's at the top and bottom—but zeroing in on the in-betweens can tell you something too).

Look closely at your Client Avatar—then take a few minutes on each client, envisioning each one and comparing them to your ideal. Who is hitting the mark? And who is essentially draining your finite resources to serve them?

Don't panic if your current client list has only a tiny percentage of your ideal clients. The key here is to dial into who you want to serve and start pruning the bad fits while replacing them with your sweet-spot people.

Sometimes you have to prune right the heck now. Like Michael R. who found himself in an untenable situation, you may have to fire a client so that you can breathe. Or maybe showing a couple of problem clients the door will change your work and life for the better in a nanosecond.

A word of caution here. You can fire clients thoughtfully and politely—essentially saying, "It's not you, it's me," and both walk away on good (or neutral) terms. What's only rarely possible is getting *them* to change when what you're already doing is working for them. It's far easier to set your terms and boundaries with new clients than to change them with already happy clients.

Like the consultant who decided to convert his freelance-style practice to a strategic retainer only. Great idea—it suited him and his target market, and he'd built the reputation to carry it off. He even attracted his first two retainer clients. But instead of trying to find a happy medium with a whale client he liked, he presented his new model as a take-it-or-leave-it decision.

They felt blindsided and showed him the door the next day—cutting off 75 percent of his revenue in an afternoon. Had he simply started a discussion to test the waters or waited until he'd had a couple more new clients, he'd have had a smoother transition. Lessons from this story: Think through all your actions from the client's side before you pull the trigger, and don't put 75 percent of your marbles all in one place.

Look, I get it. Cutting off ANY client when you're not making your nut is an exercise in terror. I'm not telling you to go there if you can't buy groceries or keep a roof over your head. Just know that in the long run, focusing your efforts on the right people and quickly turning away the bad fits is an investment in all of your bottom lines: financial, intellectual, and emotional.

Do your concerted best to get rid of the bad fits as soon as you can reasonably do so. I once worked on retainer for the longest two months of my life with a high-profile author-consultant-speaker who hadn't quite figured out the art of treating people as actual humans.

The day I had to listen to a screaming match between him and his spouse while we were trying to strategize his speaking business was the day I quit. It was summer, I had only two other clients, and my hubby was between gigs. But I let that client go (nicely), and another one popped up a few days later and then another one after that. The universe rewards action.

"Find a group of people who challenge and inspire you, spend a lot of time with them, and it will change your life."
—Amy Poehler

I feel this way about my private coaching clients, and it's the hurdle they have to jump to work with me. In addition to needing precisely the skills I bring to the party (so they're getting great value from our work together), I'm looking for clients who challenge and inspire me too—pros who are bright, action-oriented, and care a lot about their work and their impact on those they serve.

Naturally, they want to make more money. Who doesn't? But once they get to a certain point, it's less about the money and far more about how they spend their time, about the impact they want to make on their world—the revolution they want to lead.

I can always tell I've met a potential client when I fall in love with their ideas and big goals—when I get as excited as they are by their dreams, actions, and triumphs. When you work intimately with clients, and you're midwifing big transformations, an emotional connection between you is what makes those great outcomes possible.

It's often said that we are the sum total of the five people we hang out with—if that's true, then what do your top five clients "say" about you? Would you shout from the rooftops about them and your work together, or hope you don't ever have to cop to knowing them?

One of my favorite clients was an incredibly savvy, visionary CEO with a massive mandate for change. Their board was involved in our strategy and was forward-thinking and astute. While the project had its challenges, it was the single best team project I ever assembled or was a part of. I would have walked through fire to get us all where we'd promised to go.

It's no surprise that the CEO and I bonded over this project. I'll never forget sitting with them and a board member in a rental car in Detroit, discussing how we'd make Phase 2 work. I couldn't spend much time on-site since I was running my firm back in Chicago, so I suggested maybe we should scale back my involvement. They weren't having that and asked for more creative options.

I explained what I'd need: Committee meetings scheduled so that I traveled no more than once every two weeks—check. A project team of two colleagues to travel with me so that I could focus on strategy only and hand off the execution work—check. And a mid-project break for an already scheduled vacation—check.

It wasn't until I was back on the plane that I realized I probably could have asked for the moon and they'd have figured out a way to get it for me. Because that's what happens when you choose your best-fit clients and you energize and inspire each other. I'd have been fine stepping away if we couldn't meet their needs—

and they knew that, so they not only were willing to be flexible, but they trusted me to keep their best interests in mind.

All this is to underscore that choosing your ideal clients—those who energize and inspire you—is your single most critical task to position your authority business. When you make wise choices, you ensure that your business isn't just profitable but happy. That you no longer wake up wondering how you're going to get through the day, but can't wait to get going. Your best days will start with "Wow—I can't believe I get to do this today!"

With that thought firmly in your head, let's move on to why and how to specialize so you can build a niche that is your own.

Takeaways on your ideal client:

- It's not about how much money your clients have, but whether you are inspired and energized to serve them.

- Building your own business vs. working at a job means you are in charge of who you spend your time with.

- You'll find your first clue into who you'll work with best by looking at your past experiences where you were jamming on all cylinders.

- Until you know who you want to attract, it's tough to fill your pipeline consistently and reliably with ideal clients and buyers.

- The voice you use—in person and in any marketing collateral or interviews—needs to speak to your ideal client.

- Letting a bad-fit client go is a service to both parties—regularly pruning your client list ensures you stay happy and deliver your best outcomes.

CHAPTER 4

NICHE: BECAUSE YOU DON'T BECOME A HERO BY BEING LIKE EVERYBODY ELSE

"You gotta keep trying to find your niche and trying to fit into whatever slot that's left for you or to make one of your own." —Dolly Parton

Niching is a bit like putting on your Superman cape—the second your people see that big *S* emblazoned on your chest, they know you've come to help and precisely where you'll lead them. So what exactly is niching?

Think about it like this: Your ideal clients (from the last chapter) are your target market—and your niche is the specialty expertise you offer them. Naturally, you can slice and dice your expertise in multiple ways, depending on your talents and passions and the market for them.

The two most common forms of niche specialization for authority business builders are horizontal and vertical. *Horizontal* is your functional expertise—say, recruiting or finance—while *vertical* is your industry expertise, like hospitality.

When I start talking niching with certain people (you know who you are), inevitably, I get an eye roll and a response along the lines of, "But focusing on just one thing is boring!" The best comeback I ever heard was from one of our podcast guests in the pre-show chat, who remarked, "You know what isn't boring? Getting rich!"

Here's the thing: If you want to build an *authority* business with any sort of staying power, niching is nonnegotiable.

When clients and buyers want big transformations, they're not looking for a dabbler. They don't seek out Freddy at the gas station to point them in the right direction; they're looking for an expert. And when it's a considerable bet-the-business or bet-your-life problem, they're looking for THE authority.

Imagine you are the CEO attempting to merge two giant mobile communication companies. Wouldn't you spend whatever it takes to find the top expert on navigating FCC merger approvals? Heck, even if THE authority is ten times more expensive, they'll get you to the right place faster, with minimal complications, and you'll have the confidence that your time and money are being well spent.

Suppose your kid was getting migraines and your pediatrician (already a specialist) couldn't diagnose the problem. In that case, you'd be calling the pediatric neurologist PDQ because you're not taking any chances with your precious child.

We all look for experts when we want advice—and we are even willing to make some sacrifices if our pain or the potential reward we seek is big enough. When you're at the top of the heap, not only can you command premium fees, you'll likely have a backlog of your ideal clients clamoring to work with you.

The Advantages Of Niching

Niching wisely has quite a few advantages to the authority business builder:

You're instantly more memorable (and visible) than a generalist. Who will you recall a week after meeting them: the CPA who works with Broadway actors or the accountant who tells you he does income taxes?

You can make geography entirely (or almost) irrelevant. If you're an expert in a compelling enough niche—like a software developer who focuses on war games—you can sell to your ideal client anywhere on the planet, which also means you can pretty much live wherever you please (and stay off airplanes).

You can work less and get paid more. As an expert in your niche—never mind the top authority—you are in a position to charge premium fees AND design how and when you most want to work to maximize your revenue for time spent. You choose the balance of work vs. the other things you want to do with your time.

Specializing is an ideal way to indulge your curiosity. Instead of being bored by niching, the people I know are profoundly curious about their people and their expertise. They want to figure out how to get bigger, better, faster outcomes or engage more people in their revolution.

It's easier to grab attention for your work. Others in your space (or niche adjacent) are intrigued by specialists. Think bloggers, podcasters, and niche media who will be thrilled to share your message when it benefits their audience.

You can work in your genius zone. Choosing a specialty doesn't nail you to the wall, requiring you to perform a certain way. You've got the flexibility to design a business model that positions you at your highest and best value to your audience.

Have I convinced you yet?

Maybe the story of "Gus" will give you another incentive to niche. In California—especially in the big cities—chiropractors are on every corner. Competition is fierce, overhead is high, and capturing a decent slice of the local market is essential to survive.

Gus cares deeply about his clients and genuinely wants them to get better faster. A big believer in multiple treatments, he taught me exercises to do at home and incorporated a machine I've never seen (before or since) that worked wonders on my aching back.

As we got to know each other, he explained the challenges in growing his business—some were related to the abysmal insurance reimbursement rates, but most had to do with keeping a steady stream of high-paying clients. He was frustrated with last-minute cancellations and no-shows, not to mention continued patient pushback on his per-treatment fees.

Then one day, while waiting in his office, I was shocked to recognize a world-class sprinter who had just won a major event. Turns out, my outwardly modest chiropractor had a specialty in treating runners. And not just any runners, but Olympic contenders—professional athletes. He'd developed his specialty by working on injury recovery with bodybuilders (he was one himself) who wanted less pain and more mobility without drugs.

He not only studied everything he could find on the topic, but he was also experimenting with new ideas and treatments. He was close to completing a book on his findings, and he had a small fan club clamoring for it.

Yet here he was, being nickeled and dimed by people who just wanted any old chiropractor, not a master of athletic performance. I couldn't resist pointing out the obvious: Why not double down on the Olympic hopefuls?

Gus had a high-visibility profile in a small elite niche—and his athletes and their coaches referred their peers to him when they were in town. But it wasn't enough *yet* to allow him to shift his focus entirely and still pay the bills. After we kicked some ideas around (and he did some market research), he decided to focus on weekend warriors. Think highly motivated, mostly runners or triathletes with deep pockets from their day jobs.

Of course, they'd be thrilled to be treated by an Olympic-level pro. Of course, they'd understand that working with Gus costs a lot more than garden-variety chiropractic treatment. And of course, they'd want more than just chiropractic work—they'd be open to yoga, Pilates, weight training, anything that might improve their performance.

After building some momentum with his new niche, he decided to rework his revenue model. He found himself an equity partner and built a specialized gym and performance studio. He brought in related specialists who are hyper-qualified and buy into his worldview. He takes a cut of their revenue (leverage), and his clients get to rub elbows with athletes as focused as they are. And—surprise—he no longer accepts insurance (or hears complaints about his fees).

Niching not only flipped his entire business model, but now he focuses on helping the people who energize and inspire him. He's happy, he's building authority in a specialized field, he's doing work that matters, and he's making a very nice living at it.

Are we now agreed you need to niche?

How To Choose Your Niche

Unless you're just setting up your business, you probably have already niched at least superficially—like doing website design for anyone who asks. Over time, you'll get less and less satisfied with what this brings you—lots of competition and price pressure (like Gus), clients who don't appreciate your work, and an intermittent flow of work instead of the consistently full pipeline you crave.

But if you've been less than thrilled about how your authority-building is catching on, maybe it's time to take a good hard look at (re)defining your niche. Know that it's not uncommon for consultants and freelancers to switch their niche a time or two on their way to authority. Usually, it's just a matter of dialing more tightly into an aspect of what started out a little too broad.

Like when I worked with "Justin," a brilliant developer. His genius lies in how easily he moves between the worlds of his clients and his hardcore developers of code who'd be happy if they never had to speak to a single client ever again. He seems to almost intuitively understand what clients are trying to achieve with their websites and digital marketing—and easily translates it to his team, who turns it into actual working sites and systems.

His problem? He'd set up his firm as a local web developer, serving businesses in his relatively small market. He worked with the local college, a couple of financial advisors, and a handful of retailers and restaurants. That brought in just enough business to keep the lights on and pay his team, but he hungered for more exciting projects. For a bigger playground.

And yet, he was very reluctant to specialize—to build a niche beyond being the fix-it web guy in his city. After all, he reasoned, he had payroll to meet, rent to pay, and a young family who was relying on his income. I'd like to say that Justin simply conquered his fear, but in fact, the universe did him a favor—his financial advisor work attracted some industry visibility and a few referrals.

New clients with viable, healthy-margin businesses all over the US, not afraid to invest in their digital real estate, started booking projects and retainers. He loved working with them, and it was mutual. He finally decided he was ready to give specializing a go.

He created specific messaging for financial advisors and began being visible where they might see him more easily. He read their industry pubs and started speaking their language—and solving more complex problems for them. His business grew faster. After a couple of years, he was doing high-value digital marketing consulting at prices his old business model couldn't touch.

His only regret was taking so long to pull the trigger.

Justin niched by taking a closer look at what was right in front of him, already starting to beat a path to his door. The same might work for you too (and I have an exercise for you if it doesn't). You start by thinking about EXACTLY who you are serving, which specific expertise you are tapping into, and what transformations you are prepared to promise.

Let's say your specialty is employee performance management—you're consulting and perhaps writing and speaking about all the ways organizations can improve how they manage employee performance. But you feel like you're just one more voice among hundreds (if not thousands). The solution? Pick a subspecialty—or a handful—and niche down.

Imagine all the different ways you might segment your expertise:

> **By type of organization:** healthcare, nonprofits, family-owned businesses, financial services, consumer products, franchises, energy, sales organizations, tech firms, professional services.

> **By client level:** VP Human Resources, VP Sales, COO, CIO, Director of HR, Director OD.

> **By client personality/mission:** new hire, embedded leader, change agent, employee-centric, strategic.

> **By problem/opportunity:** planning, monitoring performance, developing systems, compensation, rewards.

> **By outcomes:** increased employee satisfaction, lower management costs, greater team/unit performance, decreased turnover.

Not only is that just scratching the surface, but depending on the size of the potential market and how you choose to deliver your services, you could even pull one from multiple categories. For example, you could decide to target incoming VPs of human resources in for-profit health care organizations who want to overhaul their performance management system to improve employee satisfaction.

Yes, that's a mouthful, and no, you don't want to be shouting that phrase from the rooftops. But it's advantageous to have such a clear picture of your ideal client and the outcomes they will value most from you. When we talk about publishing in Chapter 7, you'll see how much easier it will be to develop strategic and tactical content when you know who you're developing it for.

It might be just the ticket to getting your work seen by a—yes, smaller—but exceedingly highly motivated audience. Your content goes to the top of the list of those who need what you're selling.

But if you're thinking, how can I afford to focus so tightly? What about the HR heads of local energy companies that won't be checking me out now? Uh, they weren't reading up on you anyway (sorry). They're too busy looking for someone who understands the unique complexities of managing teams on drilling rigs.

I know it feels counterintuitive, but to amplify your authority, you've got to narrow your focus to a niche that's *big enough* to give you some wiggle room to build the business you envision but *small enough* so you can own it. Only then can you create the kinds of human and emotional connection that lead to the client transformations—and authority platform—your expertise deserves.

Hey, I get it; committing to a niche ranks pretty high on the fear scale for most of us. The lurking dread is that you'll be alone on your soapbox, without an audience, gradually sliding into bankruptcy. But it doesn't have to be that way. In fact, niching done right is THE way to influential authority, simplified marketing and sales, AND waaaaay better than average profit margins.

The trick is to do your homework.

One cautionary example before I show you how to hone your niche into a valuable calling card: the various creatives—graphic designers, art directors, writers, and producers—that freelance with ad agencies. They represent a staggering percentage of the people producing the actual work product in many agencies.

They're working on demand, long hours with no free time to think, much less develop their ideas or audience. Then, just as they start wondering how they're going to escape this particular hamster wheel, something unexpected happens. A client campaign goes belly up. A pandemic cuts all productions for six months. The incoming agency head decides to cut costs and clear out all the freelancers.

Freelancing this way is a trap. It's a temporary solution (at best) to getting away from the soul-sucking machinations of corporate or agency life. If you want to manage your destiny, you've got to start investing in developing your own niche, monetizing it in new ways, and ultimately, building your intellectual property.

EXERCISE 6: CHOOSE YOUR NICHE

Choosing your niche means integrating the work you've done in earlier exercises with how you'll specialize, which will help us move closer to the best authority business model for you.

1. Go to the DEFINE YOUR VISION exercise. What's the problem you most want to solve?

2. Refer to your PINPOINT YOUR GENIUS ZONE exercise. Transfer your final statement here, taking one more look at all of the questions to ensure you've captured how you truly work best.

3. Go to your DESIGN YOUR REVOLUTION exercise and bring over your last statement on the revolution you want to lead.

4. Turn to your CLIENT AVATAR exercise and summarize the ideal client you want to serve here. What does it tell you about the niche you serve? What commonalities do you see in your client base that you'd like to replicate?

By now, you probably see a lot of repetition, yes? That's how we're going to bring it all together—the people, the problems, the industry, the specialties that absorb you and drive you to operate in your genius zone.

My best clients are:

The problems I can't wait to solve are:

The industry/function I serve at my very best is:

The niche that best serves my talents is:

Congratulations! You're almost there. Just one final step, although it's an important one: You want to ensure there is market demand for you and your niche.

Hint #1: There are plenty of other people playing in that general space (while not foolproof, it signals significant revenue at stake). Example: technology B2B media consultants.

Hint #2: Your target market understands your service and is accustomed to buying it in some form. Example: CMOs know they need help with digital marketing.

Hint #3: Your research points to a significant technological or demographic demand in your market in the near term. Example:

Millennials moving into senior leadership posts means a changing, more robust market for leadership development coaches.

The challenge in niching arises when you're trying to force someone who doesn't recognize a need to pay attention to you. While certainly not impossible, it's a challenge most soloists and new firms cannot finance. Tread carefully before taking this on.

The market viability of my niche is (choose one): excellent, good, uncertain.

Test-Driving Your Niche

We're going to talk more—a LOT more—about figuring out exactly what topics and subtopics fit best with your niche and the revolution you want to lead in Chapter 7. Right now is your chance to start leaning into your niche and test-driving how viable and open your new tribe is to you and your message.

One of the most tried and true ways to see how much traction your niche can generate is to talk—well, actually, mostly listen—to a handful or two of your ideal clients. You'll often get better feedback if you don't already know them (no built-in biases from your relationship), plus you're allowing yourself to make new connections.

LinkedIn is an excellent resource to find and reach out to these people—if they aren't already in your network, it's easy enough to buy a few credits to permit a direct email to your targets. Simply ask them to connect to "get your perspective on X as a Y." You'll get the best response if you can keep your questions to email or LinkedIn messaging, although obviously that doesn't allow for much nuance.

If your questions are better suited for an interview format, then use LinkedIn to see how you're connected to your targets and ask your mutual connections for an introduction. Yes, I realize that requires asking favors, but most people will be happy to perform a specific task, knowing it will help both parties. You can even make it easier by essentially giving them the wording for the request, such as:

> I'd like to interview about ten heads of late-stage start-up SaaS companies to understand how they might use media expertise to grow faster. I see that you're connected to Joanna Smith at XYZ Company—might you connect us?

Pro tip: When conducting your interviews, make it very clear you're only trying to understand their perspective; you are NOT having a sales conversation (although it might lead to one down the road). And at the end of the interaction, don't forget to ask if you can stay in touch, which leaves the door open for them to join your circle.

I've guided clients through this for countless specialties, and the feedback is universally priceless. It's pushed them in new directions, made them contract their idea to an even tighter niche, and—despite it not being a sales conversation—handed them an opportunity to propose to a potential new client.

Niching In Action: Mike And Morley

When I first met Morley Winograd and Mike Hais, they'd just published their second book on millennials (they were leaving the following week for a book tour). Since they'd just left their academic and business careers, they were thinking maybe they could build a speaking and consulting business. But so far, they'd sold a total of one speech, for the princely sum of $500 (that they would share between them)—AND they had to make a three-hour flight each way plus a stay overnight to deliver it. Not exactly the next career they had in mind.

When we dug into their messaging and digital content, we realized two things were happening. First, when they spoke of millennials, they usually positioned them by explaining a generational theory of history that says every roughly twenty years, one of four archetypal generations appears. And every eighty years, they repeat again. They were always doing a fair amount of context-setting before they even mentioned millennials. And their speeches had a little more academic flavor than they thought readily marketable.

Second, their latest book was a big idea book on all the areas millennials would impact in American society—government, leadership, education, family, and entertainment. And while it was a superb authority builder, we needed to find a way to the niche groups with generous speaking budgets. Since Mike and Morley were fascinated with—and deeply steeped in—entertainment and media, we decided to plant their flag there.

So we engineered a few changes and then took them out for a spin to test them and tweak until we hit the right sweet spot:

> They experimented with no longer talking about the four generations (except as audience icebreakers) in their speeches and marketing collateral, focusing 100 percent on millennials. This shift was a huge hit—it turns out it was enough for their speaking audience to know that they had based their conclusions on rigorous research.

They adopted a new call to action (their revolution): *Millennials are remaking America. Are you ready?* Timing was everything on this one. In 2011, it struck exactly the right tone because forward-thinking companies were trying to wrap their arms around the newest generation hitting the workforce and consuming products.

They niched down to high-profile entertainment and media leaders—developing a list of criteria to prioritize which they most wanted to reach. They decided to target the program directors of those industry conferences, of which there are many.

And, while it made them hold their breath on a few occasions, they agreed to keep raising their speaking fees until someone cried "Uncle." Nobody ever did. We bumped their $500 fee to $2,500 immediately after niching and kept increasing it. After eighteen months, they hit $15,000.

As part of their niching (and branding), Mike and Morley also focused on the depth of their research-based approach as a differentiator from some of the empty suits hitting the speaking circuit. They are committed to a rigorous, research-based practice (Mike is a PhD researcher), and their audience could firmly rely on their observations, data, and advice. One way they demonstrated this? When reporters called for quotes, they were exceptionally generous, pointing them to data to enhance their story. It was rare when they didn't become those reporters' first call next time.

In addition to speaking, they also built what they called a "parachute consulting" practice. It's a bit like speaking on steroids—they would drop into an entertainment organization for a day or two and meet with top leaders to discuss their business strategies that touch millennials. They met with network executives, cable honchos, production companies—they were even involved in conceptualizing a new TV show.

This is the success you can enjoy when you identify a tight market niche and burrow yourself in it. As you rub elbows with your people, they tell you what's on their minds—the kinds of problems they want to solve and the dreams they have for the impact of their work. You start focusing your insights, your services, and your products on your ideal client in your niche. They start reading, buying, and referring you, and the virtuous circle of authority begins.

Takeaways on niching (because you don't become a hero by being like everybody else):

- Niching is like putting on your Superman cape—the second your people see that big *S*, they know you've come to help and exactly where you'll lead them.

- Niching is nonnegotiable if you want to build an authority business with any sort of staying power.

- Your ideal clients are your target market; your niche is the specialty expertise you offer them.

- The two most common forms of niche specialization for authority business builders are horizontal and vertical. *Horizontal* is your functional expertise—say, recruiting or finance—while *vertical* is your industry expertise, like hospitality.

- When clients face a huge bet-the-business or bet-your-life problem, they're looking for THE authority, not a dabbler.

- Niching can make geography entirely (or almost) irrelevant—you can live where you like and perhaps even avoid airplanes entirely.

- As an authority in your niche, you are in a position to charge premium prices AND design how and when you most want to work.

- Niching gives you the flexibility to design a business model around your genius zone, positioning you at your highest and best value to your audience.

- Niching makes developing strategic and tactical authority content far easier and more quickly resonant when you know who you're developing it for.

- When tightly focused on a small but exceedingly highly motivated audience, you go right to the top of the list of those who need what you're selling.

CHAPTER 5

TELL YOUR STORY SO IT DOESN'T SUCK

"Because storytelling, and visual storytelling, was put in the hands of everybody, we have all now become storytellers."
—LeVar Burton

When top financial life planner Michael Kay first takes the stage on a drizzly New York night, the audience politely claps, most likely expecting some sobering words about how they should drink fewer lattes or cut the cord on cable.

Instead, he takes us back to his childhood, describing his wildly divergent and colorful parents—who could never agree about money. As he dives into the story, I can see the audience start to look at each other—*What kind of financial advisor is this?* With self-deprecating humor, he builds a picture we can all relate to: money conflict.

Heads start nodding, and when he asks about the meaning of money in their lives, the audience goes all in, calling out their responses. He keeps building momentum, weaving his own and his clients' experiences into his talk about the emotions behind money and how we have each built our own money story—and how that plays out in how we deal with money in our lives. When he finishes, the audience erupts into wild applause.

They jump up to shake his hand and share their own stories. They press business cards and phone numbers on him and can't quite bring themselves to leave the event. It takes almost an hour before he can extricate himself from the room.

He doesn't pull people into his orbit because he's a celebrity or Twitter-famous or even a recognized authority with two books under his belt. What draws people to him is the vulnerability and authenticity he reveals as he shares his story. The challenging experience of his parents arguing about money is a personal truth underpinning why he chose this work. And it's not idle self-disclosure—it's connected directly to the revolution he's leading: transforming families' relationships with money.

That is the magic of storytelling.

While we don't have enough time and space in this book to talk about all the aspects of great storytelling, we will focus on the one most critical to positioning yourself as an authority: your origin story.

How did you come to be here, right now, doing this work that matters so much to you, serving your ideal audience and helping them transition to the new world you're building?

The story you tell about how you got here allows you to let your people feel you, care about your joint vision for the future, and, ultimately, enlist with you. It's the emotional connective tissue that can create thick, often unbreakable, bonds. It's that amalgam of head, heart, and soul that ultimately pushes you beyond mere "expert" and starts multiplying your influence.

But it has to be genuine. Authentic, direct, and—even though it's YOUR story—told with the listener in mind. Your job is to connect the dots between your life experiences, your vision, the revolution you want to lead, your ideal clients, and your niche. Don't worry; I'm going to show you how.

First, let's take a look at what *Thriving Blind* author Kristin Smedley says.

> You'll see around my website here that I smile a lot. It's kind of my thing. I can find happy no matter the hell that is happening. I'm wired that way. However, there was a time that I couldn't find happy anywhere in anything. It was when I heard the words, "Your son is blind." That little sentence was a sucker punch to my heart that knocked me down for a while. I was scared. Terrified, actually. And honestly, I was pissed off. *Blind? Are you kidding me?* As if that wasn't enough, my second child was diagnosed with the same blindness three years later. A double dose of darkness.
>
> Well, not exactly. Once I learned to SEE blindness differently, my life filled with light and joy . . . and my smile returned! When I stopped seeing blindness as a barrier and instead focused on addressing the real barriers (access to the right tools, etc.), my fear, anger, and grief disappeared,

and I was able to enjoy the journey of raising three humans with unique purposes in this world. I will help you through your challenge too. I know what that unexpected sucker punch to your heart feels like. I can't take your challenges away, but I can walk with you and give you the tools I use to come through that stuff brilliant, not broken.

Not only is this a powerful story, but it's an epic through-line to her big revolutionary idea: thriving blind. She has used her story to write a book, start a movement (#thrivingblind), build a speaking and membership business, run an annual global summit, and negotiate multiple business and education collaborations. She took her lemons and turned them into strawberry lemonade.

There is one small but vital thing to keep in mind if you wish to share transformative stories publicly: you must have worked through any trauma surrounding it and be ready to put your story in service to others. There is absolutely no shame in not being ready to put your full story out there because you won't help anyone if you haven't come to terms with it yourself. Not to mention your unresolved emotion around a story has the potential to pull the focus off the vision you're creating for your audience.

Over the years, I've been privy to some very dramatic and sometimes deeply tragic stories. When your revolution is to help others overcome the same thing you did, sharing that origin story—like Kristin Smedley has done—is essential and may also be cathartic in the very best of ways.

But when your biggest story is one of loss, you may not be ready to put it front and center. "Angela" desperately wanted to switch her specialty from training to coaching (she'd obtained several coaching certifications) but had a confidence problem in her credentials. Did she have the background and experience to focus her practice on coaching and still make a living?

I was surprised at her concern since every indication I saw in working with her was that she was a natural coach, even more so than many with far more experience and credentials. As we uncovered her experiences and stories, it turns out that Angela was the only daughter of an alcoholic mother. Her job as a child was trying to get her mother to function—to go to work, participate in family life, and stay sober. No surprise that coaching was as natural to her as breathing.

We didn't use that story as part of the origin story for her business—she wasn't interested in sharing that level of personal struggle. But looking at her story in a new way gave her the confidence to pivot her business to coaching. Today, she's a highly successful and influential executive coach for women and people of color breaking into the C-suite.

But what if you don't have a dramatic story like Kristin's or Angela's that ties right into what you're doing with your life? Not to worry—you can still connect the dots by using your story to bring your ideal client a little closer to you.

My own story of starting my current business wasn't terribly dramatic. But I have to say, I struggled for quite a while to tell it in a way that was both compelling and true to my brand. Finally, in sheer frustration, I reached out to a copywriter and spent $2,500 to have her write my story—and used only one phrase from it! But I always felt that engagement was worth every penny because she helped me see and position my life up to the start of my business in a way that not only energized me, but captured my ideal audience.

Here's the story I wrote and used to great effect for quite a few years.

My Past Life

I studied business with engineers (MBA from Rensselaer Polytechnic Institute) and led introverted brainiacs at some huge consulting firms: Towers Perrin and Arthur Andersen.

I have worn the blue power suit AND the pearls. I pitched in Fortune 500 boardrooms. I made global partner—at thirty-one. But when I saw the twisty, soul-sucking machinations required to stay in the corner office, I put on my big girl panties and headed for the exit.

First stop: creating a loveably quirky company of hyper-qualified MBA moms. Qwest was a place where experts could do their best work on their terms and be celebrated for it. It landed us, among other places, on the cover of *The Wall Street Journal*.

My next move was selling the firm to Arthur Andersen and teaching them (and others) how to make flexibility work in big-firm America.

Post-Enron, I spent a year cooking, designing, and selling fine china and crystal, just to make sure I hadn't somehow missed my true calling (I hadn't).

And then, I took one last "real" job, leading a national team coaching torpedoed corporate execs into new work. Think: daily human tragedies and triumphs—humbling and potent stuff.

After one final tug at the ripcord (2007), here I am, indulging my entrepreneurial appetite for freedom, creativity, and no limits.

Can you feel the energy flowing from this? (Bonus points if you can identify the phrase from the copywriter.) It felt very risky at the time—no one from the big firms had put themselves out there quite like this and I was prepared to be ridiculed.

Instead, anyone who didn't like it simply didn't engage—and those who did moved in closer, which is precisely the outcome we want with our story.

Ironically, the only negative feedback I got from those in my previous life (I'm still not sure why I cared what they thought) was that it was risqué to pose for a photo without a jacket. Yep, I dared to show my arms! That one was easy to ignore, but the truth is, by the time I had posted my story, I no longer cared about those who didn't like it. Instead, I was 100 percent focused on the people it spoke to, since *they* were my future.

And that's my well-earned advice for you too. The only "votes" that matter are yours and those of your ideal clients and buyers. Everyone else can go pound sand.

Discovering Your Story

One of the few reality TV shows I always tuned into was *Who Do You Think You Are?* They'd pick a celebrity and someone on their ancestral family tree and track down their story. And they used this tagline: "Discover the story that led to you."

Well, that's what we're doing here, except you're discovering the story that led to your work—what you're doing and who you're serving. Because making sense of those past experiences is a critical component of developing a compelling authority business.

You begin by understanding your past; defining experiences that have shaped you and formed the arc of your career. Before you can even start to write your story—in your bio, on your website, in social media—you need to get very clear on the experiences that have shaped and defined you.

EXERCISE 7: YOUR DEFINING EXPERIENCES AND STORIES

You can build powerful emotional connections with your ideal audience by capturing the unique experiences—in the form of stories—that have marked how you got to where you are right now. For this exercise, you're going to briefly outline some of your most memorable personal and professional experiences. Write as many as you like, but be sure to include at least ten situations.

One way to start is to be very linear; start from your earliest memory. So let's say you remember being four, and your brother took your favorite monkey toy and shredded it. Write that down as #1. Maybe after you're all done, you learn that that experience made you not want to share and ultimately work as a soloist. Or maybe it means absolutely nothing. But if you don't write it down, you can't connect the dots later.

What else happened in your childhood? Where did you grow up? Who were your friends? How did your family get along? What were your hobbies and sports and influences?

And then start remembering the things you did in and around your school years—art projects, building model airplanes, acting in plays, conducting science experiments. Try to capture all the different interests that intrigued you up through high school. And note any key relationships that mattered to you—teachers, scout leaders, your grandma. People who wrote on your slate early.

Then segue to your college years. Did you have a gap year? Be sure to explore that too. Note the jobs or internships you held in college—what did you learn? What courses jazzed you? Try not to attach too much judgment here. Your job is to get the essence down—you will decide later if and how it played into the rest of your life.

And then we have your work years. In addition to noting the jobs you've held, think about the significant (to you) projects you contributed to or led. Did you love them? Hate them? Learn insane amounts from them? How did they lead to what was next for you? What kind of people brought out the best—or worst— in you?

Keep at this—preferably in multiple sittings—till you can read through it and feel like the most important highlights/lowlights of your life and work are there.

You can stop there if you like, but if you're not a purely linear thinker, you may want to get a tad more creative. Instead of focusing on time frames, pick some aspect of what you love to do. What are you doing when you're in your genius zone—where everything runs on all cylinders, and you lose track of time?

Let's say one of your "things" is deep analysis; maybe you're a financial whiz, and you like to start your big projects with an in-depth financial review of your client's books. When else in your past did you do that kind of work? Where does that come from? Looking back, you may remember helping your mom balance the family budget or your first accounting class where you had an "aha!" moment. Or maybe it was researching car parts to fix the family car with your dad.

Explore each of your work and life loves in that fashion, and be sure to outline at least ten defining experiences.

How Much Gravity Spells Authority?

By now, you'll have some clear insights into the defining moments of your life. But before we go any further, I want to make a point about the gravity of your story. Yes, you'll need a certain amount of gravitas to build an authority business, but that looks different on every person.

And this is where story comes in. Even a Nobel Prize-winning physicist makes themselves and their work more accessible by telling their story. What made them dedicate their life to their craft? Where did their curiosity come from? How did their most game-changing insights break through?

Story is how we make our work more accessible, more memorable, more sticky. From manga graphic design to coding war games to nuclear engineering, sharing our story allows us to expand our impact on the people we most want to reach.

Your story doesn't have to be cute, inspirational, or even clever; it just has to hit your audience right between the eyes and 100 percent fit with your style and expertise. For example, take journalist Errin Haines, who uses this traditional but powerful bio on her site:

> Errin Haines is a Founding Mother and Editor at Large for The 19th, a nonprofit, nonpartisan newsroom covering the

intersection of women, politics and policy, and an MSNBC Contributor.

An award-winning political journalist focused on issues of race, gender and politics, Errin was previously the *Associated Press'* National Writer on Race and Ethnicity. She has also worked at *The Washington Post, The Orlando Sentinel* and *The Los Angeles Times.*

Errin was a Fall 2019 Ferris Professor at Princeton University, teaching a class on black women and the 2020 election. She joins Georgetown University's Institute of Politics as a fellow in their fifth anniversary class in Fall 2020.

Originally from Atlanta, Errin is based in Philadelphia with her dog, Ginger.

See how she has woven her big idea passion project (The 19th) with a gravitas-packed list of major news outlets, publications, and universities? Only a tiny glimpse into her personal life, but this feels like exactly the right balance for her.

Yes, your story must have enough gravity to give your message and vision substance. Just don't fall into the trap of thinking that means you've got to channel the "Anyone, anyone?" teacher in *Ferris Bueller's Day Off.* While lightly and humorously told, Kristin Smedley's story still carries the weight of gravity because of her deep experience.

Writing The Story Of You

From the YOUR DEFINING EXPERIENCES AND STORIES exercise, you'll have some clear insight into the defining moments of your life. So now, let's talk about what your origin story—the story of you—*must* have not to suck.

There are many storytelling models that you might follow. Still, when it comes to origin stories for authorities, my favorite is from Dr. Dennis Rebelo's *Story Like You Mean It: How To Build And Use Your Personal Narrative To Illustrate Who You Really Are.* His model, which I'm borrowing here to talk about origin stories for authorities, has three parts: your hero story, your collaborative story, and your virtuous story.

Your hero story, like author Joseph Campbell's hero's journey, is about how you've overcome an obstacle. It might be dealing with a sudden dramatic event life decided to hand you—like Kristin Smedley. Or learning the Japanese language and culture when you were ten and your family moved overseas; becoming the breadwinner at thirteen when your dad left; proving your mom wrong when she said you'd never make it as a writer (talking to you, Quentin Tarantino).

Your collaborative story is about working with others. You're teaming, demonstrating guts, grit, and courage working toward a common goal. This story shows your reader that you not only attract others, but you are dedicated to something bigger than yourself.

Your virtuous story is when you're at the peak of your experience— you're in flow serving your ideal clients, moving them toward your vision for the future. (Rebelo compares this to Maslow's top hierarchy of need—where you feel you're working at your highest, best use. I call it working your genius zone.)

The story of you takes those three pieces—your hero's journey, your collaboration with others, and your virtuous story—and weaves them together. For example, if you visit Kristen Smedley's website, you'll see the arc of her origin story. I'm shortcutting it here using my own words so you can see how this works in its most simple form:

> When my son was diagnosed as blind, my dreams for him ended and my entire world shifted. I was angry. But when I started advocating for him it changed my perception of blindness—I realized he could thrive even though he was blind. So, I launched a collaborative mission to fund research and resources (we raised over $1 million and negotiated business support alliances) and was invited to testify to the FDA for a specialized gene therapy. Today, I mentor families living with blindness and speak all over the world so that we can all thrive blind.

What makes this a powerful story? First, there is conflict—in this case, blindness. Heroes must have a conflict to battle, which is where authority builders sometimes go wrong. A story with 100 percent smooth sailing—"Look how smart I've been since birth, and I just kept mastering this stuff, so let me help you too"—has no hook, no emotional appeal. You might as well hand them a résumé.

Kristin also collaborates and shows the virtuous outcome she's striving toward—working with grit and determination toward her shining vision of a world where loss of sight doesn't diminish quality of life. The other thing she's done very well, although it's invisible if you don't know to look for it, is that she has thoughtfully considered her intent in telling the story and how it relates to her vision, message, and business.

Think about your intent as you prepare to choose which stories you'll weave together to tell the story of you. What do you want your audience to *feel*; why is this relevant to them? You're not telling this story for personal catharsis—you're telling it to help move your audience toward your vision.

So, let's tackle your story! I promise this is going to be more fun and illuminating than you probably imagine right now.

EXERCISE 8: THE STORY OF YOU

Step 1: Go to your completed YOUR DEFINING EXPERIENCES AND STORIES exercise. Reread each one and start marking them as hero, collaborative, or virtuous (a few won't be any, and that's OK; they might yet serve you later to add color to your story, so don't delete anything). If you haven't got an assortment, don't panic. It just means you need to dig a little deeper into your life on the planet so far. See my suggestions above to sift through your life for the gems that impacted you, for better or worse.

Step 2: When I did this for clients, I'd do it on my screen, sort the events chronologically, and then use the highlighter to emphasize the pieces I thought might wind up in the end story. By highlighting, you're tricking the eye to help you see just the crucial call-outs. And, of course, you can cut and paste to your heart's content.

Step 3: Look for the stories within the stories. In this example, pulled from my early life experiences, I found a hero story, can you see it?

- Born in France to Americans, while my dad was stationed in the Army.

- Grew up in central Connecticut, spending every other weekend with my beloved grandparents, in part to escape chaotic home life.

- The day my dad told me he was moving out.

- When we had to move from our little house where I grew up to another school district.

- The first time there wasn't enough to eat.

- Working at a variety of babysitting and cleaning gigs to buy food and the occasional girly do-dad.

- My first paycheck job at McDonalds. I got paid for waiting on people and being hyper-responsible which was a foundational part of my nature.

- Winning honorable mention in a statewide creative writing contest.

- Leaving home at seventeen and still finishing high school with my peers.

- Started managing the breakfast shift at McDonalds, working 5:30 a.m. to 2 p.m. six days a week. Cleaned an office one night a week and worked at Subway two to three nights a week, 8 p.m. until 2 a.m. Sold Avon products door-to-door. Took full load of college classes (including summer) in between jobs for a year.

- Applied for and won a grant plus loans to finish undergrad in three years. Slept on a relative's coach for six months until I could afford a tiny apartment.

The hero story was beating the odds from a chaotic, messy, poor beginning, getting into college, and graduating in three years. I choose not to use this particular hero story because later stories were more pivotal to my work. But once you see one hero story in your own life, you'll see more. When and how did you overcome the odds to do something that mattered to you?

Step 4: Play with various combinations of your hero, collaborative, and virtuous stories. You're looking for the right combination that hits on the work you've done in the previous four chapters. As you look at each possible origin story, ask yourself:

Is where the passion for my vision came from obvious?

Does my story inspire others to trust me and believe in the revolution I'm leading?

Can others see why I care so much about making life better for my ideal clients?

Have I shown how I'm different from anyone else in my space?

Step 5: Build out your story. Building out your story means not just combining the three types of stories into one but adding some color. If you need inspiration, compare my simple outline of Kristin Smedley's story with the one she wrote and shares on her website.

Color is what takes the bare bones of our stories and makes them spine-crackingly real. Use action verbs and descriptive words to evoke authentic emotion. A little drama—when it's real, and used sparingly—can make your story sticky.

Just beware of echoing a version of what's become annoyingly common in digital spaces: a trite rags-to-riches story. A quick scroll of the ads on your Instagram feed should give you plenty of examples like this: "I was $500,000 in debt but made $3 million from this amazing secret, and I will teach it to you . . ."

That is not an authority-building message. Your best origin story ties the story of you to where you're taking your audience. With the right amount of depth, with honor, maybe even with humor. Treat it as an invitation to join you, learn, grow, and accomplish something amazing together.

Takeaways on telling your story so it doesn't suck:

- The story you tell about how you got here—your origin story—allows you to let your people feel you, care about your joint vision for the future, and, ultimately, enlist with you.

- Your job is to connect the dots between your life experiences, your vision, the revolution you want to lead, your ideal clients, and your niche.

- When your revolution is to help others overcome the same thing you did, sharing your origin story is essential (and may also be cathartic in the best of ways).

- You can build powerful emotional connections with your ideal audience by capturing the unique experiences—in the form of stories—that have marked how you got to where you are right now.

- Story is how we make our work more accessible, more memorable, stickier.

- Your story doesn't have to be cute, inspirational, or even clever—it just has to hit your audience right between the eyes and 100 percent fit with your personal style and expertise.

- Your origin story takes your hero's journey, your collaboration with others, and your virtuous story and weaves them together into a powerful narrative.

– – – – – – – – –

We've now covered the most important decisions you'll need to make when positioning yourself and your authority: your vision, the revolution you want to lead, your ideal clients and buyers, your niche, and your origin story.

It's hard to overstate the importance of positioning *before* you decide how to monetize your business and then actually sell your work to clients and buyers. Positioning yourself and your firm is the SINGLE most important thing you'll do in your business.

You've got to be willing to stake your claim on one thing—one vision, one idea, one client base, and one specialty—and then weave it into literally everything you do. It will set the stage for how, and with whom, you spend your time. And it will influence, over and over again, the right clients, buyers, and centers of influence to seek you out.

Your work—and growing your business—will get easier because everything you do is aligned and working on your behalf. And most importantly? You get to work with the people you most love to serve, making your joint world a better place.

So let's move on and I'll show you how to monetize this positioning you've carved out for yourself.

CHAPTER 6

MONETIZE YOUR EXPERTISE

"The secret of my success is that I make other people money. And, never ever, ever, ever be ashamed about trying to earn as much as possible for yourself, if the person you're working with is also making money. That's life!" —Simon Cowell

The reason we haven't talked about monetizing your expertise before now is that I want you first to be exquisitely clear about what you're bringing to the table. I want you to feel confident about what you do, who you do it for, and why it matters—the transformations you're making in the world.

Because optimally monetizing your expertise requires confidence in yourself and your mission. You must deal from strength along with a genuine, deeply felt desire to help your ideal clients and buyers. To Simon Cowell's point, there is no room for shame around being a healthy earner, most especially when you're helping your clients achieve major transformations.

You'll notice we're not talking yet about how you're going to sell your services and products—and for a very good reason. Selling should follow, not lead, how you decide to position and monetize your expertise. You can't build a sales model until you know what you're selling and to whom. Just trust that we'll be covering this in detail. I promise.

In this chapter, we're going to design the business and revenue model that will optimize your earnings, help the people you care most about, and further your mission, all while keeping you working smack dab in the center of your genius zone.

One more point here before we dive in: monetizing in this way means you guarantee your freedom and independence; it means never having to go back to working for "the man," swapping your time and headspace (much less your soul) for a paycheck. It means staying firmly in your genius zone and putting your best talents to work in service to the world. Heady stuff, right?

So let's talk about how you will optimize your revenue and profit through your business and revenue model. Many of us use those terms interchangeably, so let's start by defining them for the purposes of this book.

Your *business* model is your plan for making money.

Your *revenue* model is how and what you charge.

The distinction isn't particularly important in authority businesses as long as you always look at them in combination. It's not enough to plan or to execute—you must do both.

Let's take an example:

Jerry is a PR pro serving biomedical start-ups with a fee-for-service business model (his client pays a fee and gets certain services or outcomes in return). He works exclusively on retainer, charging different amounts depending on the client and the work involved.

Jerry's *business model* is a solo fee-for-service (no employees or contractors). His *revenue model* is a retainer, and his per-client fees currently run from $5,000 to $10,000 per month.

Note that Jerry can decide to change the amounts he charges without changing his entire business model. Or, he might decide to add employees or contractors to leverage his time. He could even choose to monetize the speaking he's been doing at conferences (another fee-for-service revenue stream) as his reputation keeps gaining traction.

If you haven't already figured this out by looking at Jerry or any of the highly visible authorities you follow, you have almost infinite choices of how you can monetize your expertise. The trick is to pull the right elements FOR YOU and assemble them into a masterful whole that allows you the optimal combination of time, money, and happiness.

The best place to start is where you are right now: how you're currently monetizing your expertise and how well (or not) it's working for you.

EXERCISE 9: YOUR BUSINESS AND REVENUE MODEL

Now that you know exactly how you want to position yourself, it's a good time to be sure you understand precisely how your underlying business is currently producing revenue for you. How do you make money right now? Does that support and optimize your (new) positioning? What changes, if any, might better align your pricing with your positioning?

Understanding your business and revenue model is a necessary and deep exercise, so please refer to the Workbook, which will guide you to lay out your detailed business and revenue model. We'll take a look at your current reality—fees for service and revenue from workshops, membership, and products—and where you most want to go.

Once you've finished the exercise, I want you to step back and take a look at the structure of your business by revenue line. How much of your revenue requires your presence to deliver? How often and how intensely are you required to be part of the work? Where have you built leverage into your model to start decoupling your time from your revenue?

Like many of those mentioned in this book, a traditional authority business model has some combination of consulting, speaking, and books as their primary revenue streams. The challenge? Unless you're a genuinely best-selling author (meaning you're making serious money from your book sales), you're locking yourself into a high price tag, low volume enterprise.

Take a look at how my client "Atticus" had structured his six-figure practice when we first met:

> **Consulting:** Average project of $125,000 with two to three projects per year (three to six months' duration).

> **Speaking:** Eight to twenty engagements per year, averaging just shy of $20,000 each.

Books: Two well-selling evergreen books (usually about 20,000 copies per year, primarily purchased by his speaking and consulting clients).

Total Revenue: Usually ranges from $450,000 to as high as $650,000, but rarely dips below $300,000.

Atticus's practice is not easy to sustain since he has very little leverage—his books are conventionally published, and royalties are a tiny piece of his income. Since his consulting is usually to CEOs and their direct reports, a few in-person visits—hopping on a plane—are expected. Ditto with speeches. And should his current books stop serving as the right calling cards, he'll have to carve out enough time to write another.

While highly lucrative when it's working, this model is a delicate balance with each income stream working in harmony. Should anything happen—say a pandemic or an extended illness— Atticus is in trouble. And, very little of his time is flexible since he's constantly at his clients' beck and call. He can't even sell the business since it's worth zero without him.

Well, you might say, for a half million-plus dollars per year, I could handle that for a few years! And chances are you could— but that practice didn't start where it is now. Instead, Atticus spent ten years on his own, writing books, making significantly less to get where he is right now. And as attractive as his income appears, it's a trap: a gilded hamster wheel.

Atticus was tired of the road, snappy with his family, and ready to shift gears. He wanted to diversify his revenue streams and "de-risk" his entire business model so that it wasn't dependent on his working like a dog. And while he'd happily choose to earn less if it freed up some time, our goal together was to keep total revenue roughly the same but change how—and how much—he worked.

How might Atticus change his business and revenue model, assuming his positioning remains the same (since that's working for him)? He has quite a few options given his tight audience of C-suite people in highly visible companies:

He could raise his consulting fees and do fewer projects— just enough to keep his hand in and his name circulating.

He might develop an advisory retainer to former clients that he primarily delivers virtually (they are large companies with generous budgets).

He could develop a piece of his intellectual property into a salable service or product.

He might decide to license his unique process to a select handful of seasoned consultants and take a piece of every deal.

He could hire employees or contractors to complete chunks of each consulting project, giving himself less revenue but more time.

Instead of traveling the speaking circuit so intensely, he could design a high-end experience for his target audience. That could look like a small group *virtual* workshop, mastermind, or exclusive community. (He might still want to speak some to keep his name and ideas in motion.)

He could write another book, this time self-publishing (so he keeps more revenue) and designing a new ecosystem around the book—perhaps a seminar or group program designed for the next level down from the C-suite. Or he could price the book more like a high-end product with multiple price points, turning a small revenue stream into a large one.

He might even try just one tweak—value pricing his consulting services instead of his static project pricing model. (When we experimented with a new client, he doubled his fee without working more.)

The beauty of monetizing your expertise is that there are no hard and fast rules, just the opportunity to experiment and adjust, experiment and adjust.

Value Pricing

Did you notice how I slipped in Atticus's value pricing option right at the end? That's because I wanted to be sure you saw the easiest, fastest way to change the financials of your business when you're providing services. You can try it with your very next new client and perhaps double, maybe even triple, your usual fee.

Value pricing is when you anchor your price(s) to the value the client places on the outcomes you're delivering. The greater the value, the higher your price. Are you helping them grow a revenue line, reduce manufacturing defects, improve call response times, sell more products on their website?

When you help them dial into their most important reason for hiring you (and don't be surprised if they hadn't thought of it in those terms before), you create a shared vision of what you will accomplish together.

And from a pricing standpoint, your price is now anchored in something they truly value and can articulate, rather than how many hours you work or a flat project rate that means nothing to your client but a budget line item.

Having the value conversation is refreshingly simple, although it may feel awkward at first. Your goal is to help the client translate what they're asking you for into an outcome that THEY assign a value to:

> Client: "We need help getting our product teams to work better together."
>
> You: "Why is that important to you?"
>
> Client: "Well, lately they've been at odds, and it bogs down our product development cycle—it takes longer to get new products in the hands of our customers. It's really frustrating."
>
> You: "So by getting your product teams to work better together, your products will get to market faster. How will that impact XYZ's bottom line?"
>
> Client: "We're not sure exactly—but we believe that we could shave at least three months off our development time if we could solve this problem."
>
> You: "OK, so that means you'll start earning revenue on that product three months sooner. What's your starting revenue for new products in their first few months?"
>
> Client: "It varies, but the average is probably around $2 million."

Bingo! Your client has just given you a top-end for your fees. Now, of course, they're not going to pay you $2 million to save $2 million—that would be crazy. But now that you've anchored them in saving $2 million, charging say $200,000—or 10 percent of that—seems like a relative bargain.

Not every project can or should be value-priced, but if you're delivering significant bottom-line outcomes, you'll want to explore whether—and how—this can work for you.

While we don't have time here for a deep dive into value pricing, you can learn more about it from our podcast, *The Business of Authority* at *www.rochellemoulton.com/podcast*. You can also check out the book *Hourly Billing Is Nuts: Essays on The Insanity of Trading Time for Money* by my friend and podcast cohost Jonathan Stark.

If you're already running an authority business providing B2B services and you're unhappy with your revenue, value pricing is an excellent place to start.

Embracing Leverage

But let's say you're just getting started with your authority business. You have even MORE options than our friend Atticus. While he chose a low-leverage authority model, you might start at the opposite end of the spectrum, creating high-leverage offerings. Of course, that means you'll need an audience big enough to buy your products and still earn you a living, but the beauty part? You might just be surprised how you can leverage even a small number of your people.

Some examples:

A slack channel-style membership designed for CXOs (choose your specialty and/or industry) to have conversations with their peers. I've seen revenue from these in the mid-six figures more than once, so it's a viable income stream. Plus, it's relatively easy to layer on other options—private masterminds and the like—to push your total revenue into seven figures. It can take a while to build, but once you hit the tipping point, you can focus exclusively on creating an excellent membership experience.

Productized services, such as "website in a day" or assessments, are usually designed for smallish businesses to get access to designers and/or developers who couldn't otherwise work at this price point. What's great about this particular service is everyone knows what they're buying from the name alone.

Regular workshops, seminars, masterminds, or memberships where you teach an aspect of your expertise to groups of people simultaneously. Ideally, you build in some sort of community component which helps people stay connected and bring value to each other (like, say, referrals). When you give value directly (what you teach) and indirectly (what your people teach each other), you increase what your people are willing to pay for your program. My own AuthorityNation group coaching program fits this category.

Stand-alone digital training products where you teach a specific skill in some combination of writing, video, and audio. These are great when you're just getting started as long as you've niched it tightly. Selling a "sales program" means competing with over 800 million Google listings, while "how to sell your pet photography on Instagram" brings up only one real competitor despite over 100 million hits.

Books, blueprints, checklists, how-to guides where you sell a written download in a single transaction. The permutations are endless when it comes to books—you can self-publish and sell them on your site or list them on Amazon and other book sites; you can write short or long books—manifestos, essays, or big idea books. If you want to start at the shallow end of the pool, try a guide or blueprint priced in the $25 to $50 range.

Before you consider trying any of these revenue models, I urge you to evaluate one important thing: what's your genius zone? Are you happiest left to your own devices, writing and dreaming up how to teach as many people as possible? You're gonna want to build leverage so you have the time and flexibility to work the way you want.

But if you're wired to be right in the thick of things with your clients—consulting, coaching, advising, solving immediate problems—you'll always crave a certain amount of high-touch work. Even then, you can still find creative ways to leverage your business so you can have some of the flexibility and scale that come with leverage.

You'll hear many people talk about passive income—like those "make money while you sleep" ads on Facebook. When it comes to authority, the challenge with breaking products and services into "active" and "passive" is that you've got to keep your name and ideas circulating no matter what you're offering for sale— which means a 100 percent passive authority business is an illusion. I don't want you basing your business on smoke and mirrors.

That's why I prefer that we talk about *leverage* whenever we look at how best to monetize your expertise—and how to create multiple revenue streams. Think of it like this: the more leverage you build, the more income potential and time flexibility you create. And the more leverage, the more likely you're creating a salable asset down the line, even if you can't imagine ever selling out. It's always wise to build toward an exit, if only for the financial flexibility to explore something new that has captured your attention.

Your Product/Service Ladder

One way to think through how you use pricing and leverage in your business is to lay out your product/service ladder. List each of your services and products in decreasing order from the most expensive to the least.

When we do this for Atticus, you can immediately see the holes:

Custom consulting:	$125,000
Speaking:	$20,000
Books:	$20

He's not giving his people very many options, is he? They have to either pony up $125,000 or so to work with him directly, hire him to speak to their people, or buy a $20 book. Atticus needs to find other price points and packaging of his expertise so his clients' and buyers' options aren't so limited. And, of course, that will open up his opportunities to earn more while potentially creating salable assets down the road should he decide he wants to exit.

If Atticus started value pricing his consulting projects, he might do fewer of them while earning more money. And then, he could choose how to make himself accessible to clients at new price points. He might create a ladder that looks something like this:

Custom consulting	$250,000+ (actual price varies)
Advisory retainer	$100,000/year
Speaking	$20,000 (max 3/year)
CXO membership	$7,500/year
Books	$20

The above is STILL a low-leverage model, but it dramatically reduces the time Atticus spends on the road and working on his business while increasing his revenue most years.

But let's say Atticus decided he wanted to create a business he could sell, to fund some walking away money to do his next thing. Willing to create substantially more leverage, he has further options. He could license his intellectual property and teach peers how to do what he does—perhaps offering a certification program. In this case, he'd probably want to do another custom consulting project or two a year so he could train his team on them.

He might nix the advisory retainer unless he could add it to the custom engagement and position the licensee to do the work while paying him a percentage. He'd want to keep the CXO membership since that's a funnel to keep future clients coming in the door. Still, he might want to add another leveraged option or two—maybe a regular seminar he co-leads with a licensee or a new "book" with a significant upsell.

His product/service ladder might then look more like this:

Custom consulting:	$250,000+ (actual price varies)
Licensing fees:	$200,000+
Advisory retainer:	$100,000/year (20% Atticus cut)
Speaking:	$20,000 (max 3/year)
CXO membership:	$7,500/year
Seminar (co-led):	$2,500
New book upsell	$250
Old books	$20

My point in showing you a few permutations is this: the sky is the limit on how you can mix and match your products and services. It gives you the ability to increase your revenue dramatically. It allows you to change how and when you work; reach an audience subset to build for the future (e.g., you're the CXO rockstar, and you offer a program for their direct reports); and create leverage so you can work less and have more flexibility.

A comprehensive product/service ladder delivers separate revenue streams. If one gets shut off—like speaking was during COVID—you still have revenue coming in. Just like you wouldn't want one whale client as your sole revenue source, why have only one revenue stream?

There is an art to packaging (and pricing) your expertise—there is no one-size-fits-all solution or even a black box you can feed your parameters into, and BAM, the answers spit out. That means you'll want to experiment and test various combinations until you hit on the right combination for how you want to run your business.

Experimenting Pays Dividends

I was just starting to work with "Matt" when I saw he was offering an assessment option—a productized service—for $15,000 (in fact, I mentioned this on our sales discovery call). His authority levels in his niche were off the charts, so I challenged him to keep raising the price by $10,000 until he found the upper limit. He hit $25K, $35K, and now $45K without pushback. It wouldn't surprise me—given his target audience—if they'd pay $100,000 for what he initially offered for $15,000. If you don't try, you'll never know how high a value your ideal clients place on your outcomes.

I've done this same thing in my own business. When I first started doing brand strategy, I charged $2,500, including a detailed step-by-step action plan so they could implement it. I pretty quickly bumped that to $5,000, then $7,500 and $9,500.

But my most significant step (it required a very deep breath) was taking that $9,500 to $25,000 in one fell swoop. I did it for two reasons: 1) I wanted to pivot heavily toward the coaching that had become an increasingly big chunk of my business (and a pure joy), and 2) when I *do* work in a project role, I want it to be with people who are ready to invest in their success (the option now includes three months of coaching).

The result: fewer clients with higher impact and—not coincidentally—more revenue.

Sidestepping Pitfalls

Let me share some advice on avoiding the pitfalls authority builders tend to face when monetizing their expertise so that you can sidestep them:

Avoid hourly billing like the plague. While not every project is suitable for value pricing, hourly billing after your first year or two in business becomes a very slippery slope. Juniors coming up behind you will undercut your rates. Clients can't help but peruse your invoices, looking for signs you're wasting or exaggerating time. And even if you get your top rate for most of your hours, eventually, you'll hit the gilded hamster wheel.

Don't be the low-cost option. Matt's assessment was almost comically priced for someone with a long track record of major transformation in a deep-pocketed niche. You are not selling based on price, but outcomes.

Cut the ripcord early when clients push back on fees. Inevitably, a little front-end dissatisfaction with fees turns into a lot. Assuming you're delivering valued outcomes, you'll be far more content moving on to ideal clients who will happily pay your fees.

Don't let cost-centered clients twist you up like a pretzel. When longer-term clients, especially, give subtle hints about fees, you may feel tempted to toss in more services or agree to requests that aren't in your sweet spot. Resist. You don't need to feel guilty about your business and revenue model. It's kinder for everyone if you let bad-fit clients go gracefully.

Design a "whale" business very carefully. I've run and worked with some very successful "whale" practices—with a handful of key clients at any given time. As long as you're not worried about building leverage, it can be a viable authority business with two basic rules: always make sure you have at least three clients and that none is more than a third of your revenue. Of course, having some cash tucked away for a rainy day is not a bad idea either.

A Word About Money In The Bank

A consultant that had been referred to me called to discuss the expertise business he had in mind. He was debating when he could leave his (very unhappy) day job to go all in. When I asked him how many months he could go before getting a client, he said, "Maybe one."

I had the unfortunate task of explaining that, even though he was coming out of consulting and had a book of people he could call on immediately, it was unwise at best to count on a client on day one. Or day thirty, for that matter. So I asked him how much he had set aside for cash flow, emergency expenses, etc., and he said $5,000.

If he was a single guy living at home or with a pile of roommates, $5,000 could go pretty far. But he had a hefty mortgage, a non-earning spouse, and a toddler. He was in a tight spot financially to be taking big risks. And there is no way I wanted to be complicit in leading him to bankruptcy.

Instead, I advised him to reduce his expenses now—to imagine he was already inside the new business living on what he brings in—and throw as much cash as he could into a rainy day fund so he could leave his old firm with confidence.

Because having a little FU money in the bank—how much depends on your lifestyle and risk tolerance—is what allows you to say no to bad-fit clients. It lets you invest in your business without feeling like your head will explode from fear, uncertainty, and doubt. And it keeps you from making decisions for all the wrong reasons.

Do whatever it takes to squirrel away enough readily accessible cash (i.e., not in Bitcoin or the stock market) so that you can focus on building your business and taking calculated risks without driving yourself batty with worry.

With that extra peace of mind, you can comfortably explore the best ways to monetize your expertise. Using the approach and ideas I've outlined in this chapter, you're ready to experiment to optimize the mix of time you put into your business with the revenue you take out of it.

Takeaways on monetizing your expertise:

- Your business and revenue model is your plan for making money and how—and what—you charge.

- Before you can design the business and revenue model that will best monetize your expertise, you must get absolutely clear on your positioning (from Part 1).

- Monetizing your authority in the right way means solidifying your freedom and independence and never having to go back to working for "the man."

- A traditional authority business model combines consulting, speaking, and book sales as the primary revenue streams, but sticking 100 percent to that approach locks you into a low-leverage model.

- Value pricing is when you anchor your price(s) to the value the client places on the outcomes you're delivering—the bigger the value, the higher your price. It's also a speedy way to increase your service line revenue dramatically.

- Not every project can or should be value-priced, but if you're delivering significant bottom-line outcomes, you'll want to explore whether—and how—this can work for you.

- Embracing leverage allows you to decouple time worked from revenue. There is no revenue ceiling on leveraged authority businesses (you also have the flexibility to design a business that positions you firmly in your genius zone).

- The more leverage you build, the more income potential and time flexibility you create. And the more likely you're building a salable asset down the line, which gives you even more options.

- Try laying out your product/service ladder in decreasing order from the most expensive to the least, so you can see where you have opportunities to add, remove or reprice your options.

- Building a comprehensive product/service ladder delivers separate revenue streams that help "de-risk" your authority business. If one stream gets shut off you still have revenue coming in.

- Monetizing your business isn't a one-and-done. Experimenting with your options and regularly raising high-value prices allows you to find the optimal balance for your revenue, your time commitment, and how you work best.

_ _ _ _ _ _ _ _ _

Now you understand how best to position your expertise to build authority; you also have the tools to monetize it.

While you'll need to experiment to find the optimal balance that works for you, knowing that you have almost limitless options to monetize your expertise should give you the confidence to keep pushing against any perceived ceiling to your revenue.

The other benefit beyond revenue? When you discover that ideal formula, running your business becomes smoother. You have more flexibility to offload tasks you don't care to do, more time to enjoy life away from work, and the opportunity to build a salable asset that just might secure your future.

Alrighty then, let's move on to how to sell your services and products like the authority you are becoming.

CHAPTER 7

PUBLISH LIKE IT'S A REVENUE STREAM (BECAUSE IT IS)

"Nothing stinks like a pile of unpublished writing."
—Sylvia Plath

Selling authority without publishing is like trying to nail Jell-O to the wall. No matter how brilliant it was when you grabbed the nail gun, you wind up with a worthless pile of glop.

Publishing is how you make your authority visible, tangible, and sticky. It's how you float ideas and see which ones take root with your ideal clients and buyers. It's how you develop a point of view and a body of work that becomes a magnet for your people (and makes selling easier over time). And it's how you entice those with more prominent platforms to share them with you, so you both grow.

If you want to build authority, you're in the publishing business.

Thankfully, your options to develop a sustainable publishing habit are almost unlimited. The trick is to find the right combination for your brand of expertise, your audience, and your genius zone. Ideally, you will blend both writing and speaking to give you the greatest opportunities for traction (your ideas taking hold) and connection (stirring up emotion).

Writing gives your audience the flexibility to absorb your content in different ways (short form, long form, even tweets) in a format that appeals to those who learn best by reading. It's efficient— at least for the reader—and a time-tested way to get your views shared more widely on various platforms.

Speaking allows your people to connect with you emotionally; to hear your voice, how you relate to ideas and other people, see your body language. It requires them to make more of a commitment—they can probably read a podcast transcript in ten minutes, while it might take them forty-five to listen to the whole episode—but speaking pulls your people in closer.

But before we delve into designing your optimum balance between writing and speaking, let's talk about your point of view.

Your Point Of View

Your audience wants to know what you believe; they won't care enough to listen, read, or watch your stuff until you viscerally grab them with your belief system. I call it your point of view.

Think of it as building connective tissue between you and your ideal audience. Your point of view is how you think about your vision, the revolution you're leading, your ideal clients, and your niche. And until you commit it to writing, it never quite crystallizes, which means you won't develop the clarity of an authentic authority.

It's a bit like designing the world you want to live in; it will become your guide to all sorts of big and small decisions when it comes to publishing. For example, should you write about X? Align with Y? Sound off on Z?

Your point of view becomes the prism for your clients and buyers to differentiate you from the dozens, hundreds, or even thousands of choices they might make. To connect with you. To believe in you.

Your point of view should answer your audience's pivotal question: Why should I listen to you?

Let's look at a few point of view examples I developed with clients, so you can see what I mean.

For a PR consultant to nonprofits:

People power social change.

People who want to make a difference. Who want to do good. Who want to be inspired and connected. Who want to live with a sense of mission.

To make meaningful social change stick, visionaries, changemakers and innovators must connect with those emotions. They must build and engage a colorful community of supporters, evangelists, allies, funders, clients, and decision-makers.

To spark connections and deepen engagement with their community, social change leaders listen closely and act with transparency.

The very best develop deep insight into the motivations and perspectives of their community, root their communications in compelling stories, practice profound respect and embrace diversity in all its forms. They reach people where they are and motivate them by connecting with their values.

For a fashion consultant:

The XYZ woman—a confident, modern, American businesswoman—shuns excess and "trends of the minute." Whether in a board meeting, having dinner out with friends, or attending a special event, she is confident in her understated, effortless approach to style and fashion.

Never one to crave designer labels and logos to validate her fashion sense, the XYZ woman builds her wardrobe around go-to pieces that work effortlessly for her. Clean, timeless style that expresses who she is and who she is becoming.

Sophisticated, yet effortless. Striking, yet understated. True American style.

For a big brand B2B social media consultant:

The new world for brands is hyper-socialized and digitally democratized.

Brands that win (enduring and beloved brands) become part of the cultural narrative. They don't rely (solely) on paid media to build their brand. Instead, they tap into their potent cultural truth to make authentic, meaningful contributions to the culture they serve.

Brands that win must master a social mindset: they must listen, learn, truly engage, and consistently contribute genuine value to the cultural discourse of their best audience.

Just to be clear, a point of view is not a marketing piece, even though you'll probably wind up pulling a few sound bites from it. Instead, the exercise of outlining the planks of your belief system is to focus you even more concretely on what you care about, what you're committing yourself to as you build authority. And, not coincidentally, it will help you identify the lanes of content you want to develop so that your publishing leads directly to impact and revenue.

A good starting point for building your point of view—one that will stimulate your left and right brain—is to think *manifesto*. A manifesto is more than the last ravings of a lunatic or the musings of a politico. It's a written declaration of what you believe to be true, which forces you to step into the light and hold yourself accountable to your belief system.

Start with the statement "I believe" and jot down your core beliefs about your work, your people, the revolution you want to lead, and your expertise. Don't worry about the exact words; just broad-brush the concepts. Come back to it again and again until you've got your basic belief set down.

I believe . . .

I believe . . .

I believe . . .

The most important thing here is to capture the pivotal stakes of your belief system. Don't be afraid to be pithy or in-your-face if that's your style. Like the marketing consultant who used this phrase in his point of view: "If you don't ask for feedback, you are a chicken shit. Grow up." Strong words, yes, but his ideal client genuinely wanted to improve, and he'd learned the hard way that those who didn't want direct, candid feedback were bad-fit clients.

If your list of statements isn't flowing easily, try thinking about these four questions:

> **Who do you *really* want to work with?** Know that narrower is better; the more tightly you describe your ideal tribe, the easier it is to recognize each other. Use your work from the YOUR CLIENT AVATAR exercise to dial into the specifics of your people.

> **What are the tent poles of your work?** If you're a leadership consultant, what do you believe about the role of leaders in organizations? What distinguishes great leaders from the merely good? How should organizations develop their future leaders? Get clear on the belief set that underlies every assignment.

> **What outcomes are you striving for?** Think big. How will you get there if it's not on your radar? If you're a financial advisor, your goal may be to help clients live the life they've always imagined. Look at the work you've done—your best success stories—and look for the commonalities in the end result.

> **How have you structured your work to deliver those outcomes?** This question is about real, tangible aspects

of how your service delivery meshes with your promise. Drill down to **exactly** the aspects that form your authority DNA. A financial advisor who wants to help clients reach their dreams should not open a conversation asking about their investment mix.

Once you're confident you've got enough color to feel like you've captured the essence, you're ready to tackle your point of view.

EXERCISE 10: BUILD YOUR POINT OF VIEW

Now we're going to narrow all of your manifesto beliefs into a very specific point of view that no one else in your space would— or could—replicate. It's typically four to six paragraphs that you write as though you're explaining your belief system to a potential client.

1. Looking over your "I believe . . ." statements, what's the one statement you believe is always true in your area of expertise? Some examples: Beloved companies make decisions that respect and honor the customer. No one becomes a brilliant leader alone. The war for talent is just beginning.

2. Say more about your one statement. Why is it true? What factors can make that statement accurate for your clients? What gets in the way?

3. What MUST happen for your statement to become a reality? How do you take your clients from where they are now to your vision for them?

4. Now put together your statements in a series of paragraphs. The first paragraph should be your sentence from #1 above. Then add additional paragraphs, using

your ideas from #2 and #3 above, keeping each paragraph to no more than two to three sentences. If you get stuck, imagine you have one minute to describe your beliefs in your area of expertise to a potential client. Keep in mind that this exercise isn't about your technical methodology. It's about connecting your expertise and worldview with your potential client base.

Before finalizing your point of view, read it over and ask yourself these questions:

1. Have I captured the essence of my belief system?

2. Does this sound like something I would say?

3. Have I differentiated myself enough from other players in my niche?

4. When I read this back to myself, do I get excited? Is it the work that gets my motor revving?

My point of view is: _____

I know that pinpointing your viewpoint can be challenging (hey, it can also be freeing and even fun). But this is an essential step so that you're not wasting time on publishing extraneous stuff. Instead, you're dramatically spiking the odds that your writing will viscerally touch your target audience.

Know that most people flail around a bit when they first start developing content for their audience—it's perfectly normal. In fact, it's part of the process of experimenting as you test your ideas and develop your vocabulary and your point of view. Keep paying attention to what connects you with your audience and inspires them to engage—and double down on those.

Lanes Of Content

One of the many reasons I'm encouraging you to state your point of view boldly and unequivocally is because it will guide you to what I call your lanes of content: the three or four lanes where you'll be driving the content you'll be publishing.

Just like niching down to a specialty, narrowing your content lanes allows you to concentrate and focus so you can get the most leverage from your publishing. Who is more likely to attract a dialed-in audience: a financial consultant who writes about hedge funds and their shenanigans or one who writes about whatever seems interesting that day?

Restricting your content to a few lanes is the authority version of Marie Kondo's sparking joy by reducing your possessions to only what matters. When you strip off the excess, it shines the spotlight on what is truly important and, when done well, turns you into catnip to your ideal audience.

Let's take another look at our three earlier point of view examples and see how we might tease out their lanes of content.

Our PR consultant to nonprofits is about how you can't make social change stick without involving people and emotions. Given his specific hot buttons and audience, he might decide to focus his content on three lanes:

> How to connect changemakers' ideas to the emotions of their audience.

> Building a multicultural community of support for your cause.

The art of listening to and engaging with your constituents.

Note that while he's putting boundaries around his publishing, he has created profound opportunities to set himself apart in his niche AND pull in the deeply committed changemakers who are his best clients.

The fashion consultant wants to reach the "confident, American businesswoman," so she might design lanes of content that look something like this:

> How to work with the pieces already in your wardrobe to craft a timeless style for yourself.
>
> When to incorporate a new fashion trend without infringing on your already effortless style.
>
> Crafting a timeless style and wardrobe that smoothly transitions from work to social life.

Within those three lanes, she'd have the flexibility to write stories about how a specific woman dealt with one of those challenges and a variety of how-to's to maintain an effortless style as seasons and trends change. She could write predictions on where she saw fashion and style headed. Even by limiting her topics, she has created an almost endless well of potential headlines.

Finally, let's look at our **big brand B2B social media consultant** who is about hyper-socializing ideas in a digitally democratized world. He might decide to focus on:

> How brands can become part of the cultural narrative of their customers.

How brands should listen, learn, engage, and contribute value to the cultural conversations of their target customers.

How brands can master a social mindset.

See how even limiting yourself to three lanes of content still gives you so much to distinguish your authority? Especially in the case of a social media consultant (try googling that title and getting placement anywhere on the first ten pages, never mind page one). No one in that niche is tackling this idea of tapping into a cultural narrative—it's white space.

Pro tip: If you're not sure you're designing the right lanes for yourself, sit down, set a timer for twenty minutes, and start drafting headlines for possible stories. If you can come up with at least ten without trying too hard, you've probably got a winner.

What you're looking for here is a relatively open place to plant your content flag so that your investments of time, energy, and money in building your authority will pay off. Of course, that doesn't mean you'll be the only one publishing in your space— just the only one with your particular point of view and the voice you'll hone as you keep publishing.

Getting Started

Getting good at publishing your ideas is a process—and it starts with your internal commitment that this is an important use of your time to build your business. You have to cross the chasm from thinking this is something "nice to do" to "this is a critical piece of growing my business." It ranks right up there with client work—which means you schedule time to do it and say no to less strategic distractions.

I put my writing, podcasting, and thinking time directly into my calendar, and it is sacrosanct—no one is allowed to book that time, and I hold myself accountable to a set of outcomes. I know that if I start cutting corners on my publishing, it will show itself in results: slower growth in my email list, reduced membership in my programs, fewer guest invites, and eventually, lower revenue.

So let's agree you're going to commit yourself to publishing. What exactly makes the most sense for you, your audience, and your expertise? Should you develop an email list, write articles for an industry site, or start a podcast?

If you're just getting started with publishing, the quickest way to build your point of view with an audience that you "own" is with an email list. Assembling even a tiny group of people who have agreed to welcome your content into their email is an excellent petri dish to begin sharing your expertise.

When I first started my current business back in 2007, I didn't have an email list. But I did have a decent network of people I knew—and I used LinkedIn to round them up and gather email addresses for any I didn't have in my contact system. My first email went to about six hundred people—about a third of whom immediately unsubscribed because I hadn't bothered to get their permission first (a not unimportant detail—my message should rightly have been called spam). **Lesson #1: Don't take your list's attention for granted.**

I found that those who opted in would reward my efforts to understand their situation with their attention, and eventually, their wallets. I still have people on my list who joined back in

2007 and continue reading and interacting with my emails. The record longest simmering buy came from a guy—more of a lurker than a regular commenter—who purchased my most expensive option after being on my list for thirteen years! **Lesson #2: Longtime list members who still open your emails are every bit as valuable as the newest additions to your list.**

My experience is not unique in the realm of expertise and authority. When you're an expert in a carefully defined niche, your people will follow you for years. They change companies, they get promoted, they start businesses, they move across the country, but they stay connected with you. Maybe they buy, share your stuff, or just absorb it and use it to better their work and lives. How great is that? **Lesson #3: Once you find and burrow into your lane(s), your emotional connection with your list deepens.**

Today, my advice is to always start with an email list, no matter what content you decide to produce, since no one can ever take that away from you. It is a precious asset that will always prove fruitful if you nurture it. I've guided consultants to build six-figure retainer businesses from a list of under 100 people, and I've seen successful product launches (with as much as 20 percent of their list buying in) with three-digit lists. It's not the size of your list, but the quality of your connection—how well you listen and provide value that solves their problems or gets them closer to their dreams.

It's hard to fully realize the power of an email list until you have one and push that SEND button—and within minutes, you see your people responding or clicking through to your website.

I'm pretty sure I've convinced you by now, right? So if you don't already have a list, or yours is growing slower than you'd like, there are a few simple moves you can implement as you begin publishing:

> Make a compelling offer on your website to join your list—and no, an invite to "join my newsletter" doesn't cut it. Instead, offer something, usually in a bite-sized version, that addresses the main pain point of your ideal audience.

> Use social media—especially LinkedIn and Twitter—to "tease" out your ideas. Social is a distribution system that you can use to direct people to your website; send them to your content pages with a built-in juicy offer to join your list.

> Don't be afraid to sprinkle multiple offers, even for the same thing, across the pages of your site. Oftentimes, people don't see them, especially when you've buried them in the footer.

> Make everything easy and frictionless—no more than an email address/first name, a couple of clicks, and immediate delivery of your download.

> Set them up with a nurturing welcome sequence (using automation) that presents your ideal clients and buyers with an experience as close to working with you as possible.

Once you have even just a handful of list members, you're ready to rock and roll. You can write short pieces (generally 100 to 500 words) exclusive to your email list or publish the posts and then share them via email with your subscribers. (The second approach allows you to distribute those posts much more broadly—say, in social media, as an enticement to come to your website and sign up for your list).

One step up in difficulty (or down, depending on your talents) is hosting a podcast. A podcast allows you to interview—and start a relationship with—the people who most intrigue you while adding value to your audience. It instantly gives you a rich platform to begin building out your ideas, your point of view, and your comfort behind a mic.

Podcasts are pretty much the authority trifecta. And they have a very long tail—episodes are often listened to many months, even years, after their original publish date. Your audience gets to hear how you think, express yourself, and interact with others—it's like a grand preview of working with you.

Try one of those two (or swap out video for writing if that's more your medium) as your authority training wheels. They will give you priceless, low-risk feedback early on as to how your messaging and positioning resonate. Listen to how your people respond, the questions they ask, and keep using that input to better craft your content.

Winning At Social Media

Ideally, you're building your list and your social media presence in tandem. Think of social media as an accelerant to your list; use it to develop and enhance but never replace your list. Social media is a powerful publishing platform just waiting for you—they've already built it out, made it easy to use, and attracted an existing audience. The opportunity to get instant feedback on anything you publish is hardwired into the platform, which means you can keep fine-tuning your content there until it hits the mark.

Social media can be an ideal place to build your authority. Unfortunately, it's also a potential minefield if you tend to get distracted.

So let's talk about how to make it work for you with the least amount of time and distraction.

Job #1 is to find your people and attract them into the world you're building. You might start by lurking—listening in on various public conversations to understand your ideal people's worldview, challenges, and opportunities. You're trying to crawl inside their heads. Let them teach you the language they use so you can incorporate it into your content. Think of social platforms as the world's largest cocktail party; your job is to find (or create) a "room" packed with your best people.

Once you start absorbing their dreams, hopes, fears, and frustrations, your publishing—even something as small as a 140-character tweet—will start tapping into how your work can transform their lives. You'll start a gravitational pull toward you that keeps getting stronger as you learn (and share) more.

The thing to remember as you build your audience on social is that these platforms can and do change their rules regularly and without notice. That's why your goal is to entice your people to visit your website and join your email list—a piece of valuable real estate that you will always own. You don't want to build your dream home on rented land.

As you grow your base, you'll begin to build a following, and while your follower count is not necessarily a signpost of authority, it is a highly visible one. It grants social proof and helps demonstrate authority, although its weight depends heavily on your audience.

A medical doctor's patients may give it minimal credibility (do you look at Twitter before choosing your internist?), but it might be the most important factor if you're looking for the trendiest new home designer.

After you've been publishing for a while on social media and to your email list, you'll have built a small, devoted following that has helped you find your footing as a writer/speaker/thinker. Once you've got a rhythm down—you've experimented with your lanes of content and have found your voice—you are ready for prime time.

Getting Published By Others

Getting published by others feels like the holy grail. It's a tried and true way to leverage other people's platforms and grow your authority exponentially faster than you can on your own. It is simply the quickest, reliable way to get your content widely available to your ideal audience.

"Seth" published just an occasional article in an industry publication and it juiced his list by at least 100 people every time his pieces appeared. And sometimes, he'd welcome a few hundred new subscribers over a few days.

We'll talk more in the next chapter about how to get on other people's platforms. For now, we'll stick with the "what." There are so many ways you can collaborate with others in your space—or space adjacent—as well as a variety of industry or broader media outlets. Take a look at this list to spur your thinking on potential outlets for your expertise:

- Articles or columns in digital/print publications
- Livestreams and digital events

- Podcast guest interviews

- Guest blog posts

- Books or e-books offered in a joint venture

- Webinars or videos

- Quotes to journalists

- Speaking

- Industry/community presentations

- White papers

- Surveys

- Research studies

Keep it simple—start with whichever one excites you and feels like it plays to your strengths. I had a busy client do just one thing to get on other platforms: he subscribed to HARO (Help A Reporter Out) and answered every question that hit his targeted expertise. Within a few months, reporters were calling *him*, and his name was regularly appearing in specialty media publications. That exposure eventually brought him a half dozen clients that we know of and helped launch his first book.

And that's what you're after here—what works best for you. There isn't one magic formula that works for everyone. One client started with video only and amassed a loyal following before he ever wrote an actual article. Another is a terrific writer and snagged a column in his industry's must-read digital outlet by pitching an angle that fit right into his niche. They were successful because they worked within their genius zone and sought out others who could benefit from their content. Working with very low friction will allow you to find the right outlets and stick to your practice consistently.

How To Think About Publishing

An authority mindset requires thinking about publishing as a revenue stream. Even when the content sales line item in my FreshBooks was laughable, I still prioritized my publishing. Because I know that if I stop, my other revenue streams will dry up. Publishing, if not an actual revenue source (yet) for your business, still drives your growth and deserves to be treated as a revenue stream.

I often tell clients when they first start a podcast to treat it as a client engagement. Designing their show, scheduling guests, producing episodes, and—most importantly—marketing and distributing them, is a priority in building their future as authorities, which means it's every bit as crucial as client work.

The way to think about publishing is how it strategically contributes to your overall revenue. It might be something that rarely brings you direct revenue for the content you created (say, an article for *CFO Magazine*) but reliably brings you clients who pay you five to six figures per assignment. Or maybe your royalties are a relatively small line item—like for Atticus in Chapter 6— but they drive over a half million dollars in revenue.

When you look at it this way, it makes certain decisions easier. Like the consultant who was frustrated that the outlets he was writing for wouldn't pay him—he was thrilled when one finally ponied up $350 for a piece. When I pointed out that he earned $25,000+ PER YEAR from each client who came to him from those articles, all of a sudden, "free" writing looks much more attractive.

Or the consultant who sold "only" 1,000 books in the first year after launch. And yet, every one of those detailed guidebooks sold for $250. Moreover, just over half who bought them also purchased a $500 upgrade. Yep, that's a cool $375k+ just in Year 1 of an evergreen book. Do you suppose he sees his writing and publishing time as an excellent strategic investment? You betcha!

But even regularly pushing out content gems isn't enough if the right people don't see them. Publishing—like authority-building—is a team sport. In the next chapter, I'll show you how to enlist the right allies to grow your influence and impact faster than you ever could alone.

Takeaways on publishing like it's a revenue stream:

- If you want to build authority, publishing is nonnegotiable.

- Your manifesto is a written declaration of what you believe to be true, forcing you to hold yourself accountable to your belief system.

- Your point of view should answer your audience's pivotal question: Why should I listen to you?

- Articulating your point of view will dramatically spike the odds that your writing will viscerally touch your target audience.

- Narrowing to three or four content lanes allows you to concentrate so you can get the most leverage from your publishing.

- Publishing authority content means you have to move from this is something "nice to do" to "this is a critical piece of growing my business"—it's every bit as important as client work.

- If you're just getting started with publishing, the quickest way to build your point of view with an audience that you "own" is with an email list.

- Getting published by others is a tried and true way to leverage other people's platforms and grow your authority exponentially faster than you can on your own.

- Podcasts are pretty much the authority trifecta—your audience gets to hear how you think, express yourself, and interact with others—and their long tail means episodes can work on your behalf for years.

- The way to think about publishing—and decide how to invest your efforts—is to understand how it will strategically contribute to your overall business growth.

CHAPTER 8

ENLIST YOUR AUTHORITY CIRCLE—YOUR RAT PACK, APOSTLES, AND TRIBAL LEADERS

"If you want to go fast, go alone. If you want to go far, go together." —African proverb

Publishing—whatever the form—launches you into building authority. It pushes your ideas into circulation with a powerful niche and gets you in the habit of regularly producing thoughtful insights that edge your people closer to the revolution you're leading. It's your first critical step toward building your tribe of believers.

Your second step is to enlist what I call your Authority Circle—a set of three types of people that will help you expand your authority in ways that are impossible to do on your own. Unlike publishing, enlisting your Authority Circle is more of a one-to-one exercise. You're not blasting out content, but listening carefully and connecting—human-to-human—which is how we discover (and build on) resonance with our people.

Resonance is the key here. It's resonance that makes us genuinely want to see you succeed. It's resonance that powers us to make—and deliver on—generous offers, like, say, an introduction to an influential gatekeeper. And it's resonance that keeps us firmly in your camp, sharing your insights and making valuable referrals and introductions.

Who makes you feel like the best version of yourself when you're talking, writing, or listening to each other? Think of it like working in your genius zone—these are the people who bring out your best, and it's mutual. You could swap ideas or stories or enjoy brainstorming sessions for hours and never look at the clock.

There can be what feels like magic in resonance. I suggested a call with my now rat pack pal Jonathan Stark because he kept sharing my articles on Twitter. What was supposed to be a quick call turned into an hour plus of pure resonance, and within fifteen minutes of hanging up, he asked me to cohost a podcast he'd been germinating.

He had no way of knowing that I'd wanted to start a podcast for at least two years but had always stopped short because it just felt like too much of a commitment. But here was a guy who already had two excellent podcasts under his belt, and we'd do it together? Easy, yes. Magic, a.k.a. resonance, works exactly like that.

So how do you go about finding and building your Authority Circle? While it's tempting to search among the big names in your space, resist. Instead, start with who you know right now. Think of your people in three categories—your rat pack, apostles, and tribal leaders. Thinking in this way will help you give each person the right amount of attention and keep your asks in line with the level of your relationship.

Your first circle is your rat pack—those roughly in your business space where you have a high level of resonance. You may not work together directly, but you might feel inspired to team up professionally at some point (like Jonathan and me on our podcast). These are the friends you can rely on to give you their candid opinions (cheerleading or naysaying), suggest ideas for you, or just listen and respond as you ask for advice. They make introductions and do favors when asked, and you quickly and willingly do the same.

Your second circle is your apostles—the people preaching your message not because they get some advantage, but because they *believe*. They might be a very early follower (I have one who's been preaching my ideas for eleven years and counting) or one who has just converted to your point of view. They aren't passive; they're the opposite. They are sharing your published ideas with their audiences and perhaps even building on them. They aren't blind followers but thoughtful people who want to help your ideas get heard.

And your third circle is tribal leaders—people who are leading tribes of their own and who resonate with your ideas. They might have a small but dedicated following, or they could hold the keys to a large segment of your potential audience. They might align with you on just one aspect of your authority—like, say, a journalist or podcast host—because it's an idea that appeals to their audience, and they see the value you bring. Every tribal leader is unique, so each must be handled as the precious resource they are.

To develop and sustain all three types of relationships in your Authority Circle, you'll want to keep their names and needs circulating in your consciousness.

Your Rat Pack

You have had a rat pack at some point. Maybe it was a gaggle of new grads when you started your first job. Or the orientation class from your second. Perhaps it was your fellow team members on the project from hell.

Do you remember what that felt like—having at least one other person who understood your situation, who had your back and wasn't about to throw you under the bus, no matter what? When you're running an authority business, having a lively circle you can depend on (and who depends on you) makes you all stronger. Work—and life—are a little easier. You can breathe, knowing you have an outlet when you need one.

Think back to some of your work in the past. Who did you resonate with? Who felt like a partner in crime, even if you've lost touch since? (LinkedIn is an accessible resource to refresh your connections from past lives.)

Start with your innermost supporters who have always cared about your success. Not your mother (unless she's in your business sphere), but you can add close friends who are good business advisors, buddies from your previous jobs, roles, and projects.

Your Apostles

Your email list is an excellent place to start uncovering your true believers and supporters. Who consistently engages with you? Maybe they're asking questions or mentioning how they shared one of your pieces. (I keep an email folder called "Future Clients + Buyers" so I can always look them up fast.)

If you've been publishing for even just a few months, chances are you've found a fan or two on social media. Take a look at your social feeds and see who has thoughtfully vs. mindlessly shared your stuff.

Don't worry if you haven't built up any apostles just yet. They may well bubble up as you keep publishing, especially as you start to dig into your niche. The important thing here is to be on the lookout for people who start sharing. It can happen fast, like when you hit a particular nerve in your publishing, or it can be more of a slow roll, like finding your sweet spot with your new podcast.

Your Tribal Leaders

These aren't just those leaders who want to read almost every word you write, but also those niche players who may only be interested in a single aspect of your thinking. For example, maybe you're an authority on building trust in software development teams, but that Fast Company writer is only interested in your research on trust differences between failed and wildly successful start-ups.

This circle ideally is sprinkled with those you already know and your aspirational additions for the future. Who are the finest writers, thinkers, and doers in your field? And who are the up-and-coming people you are resonating with?

Think about the media outlets that could be crucial to getting you a bigger platform for your work. Who might interview you or shill your books or even seal affiliate deals? Yes, media can be a trickier "get," but if they're not on your radar, you won't be looking for ways to collaborate. Just don't get stuck on only going after the big names; small niche media with influence (current or potential) may be fertile ground for your ideas and presence.

EXERCISE 11: YOUR AUTHORITY CIRCLE

Please refer to this exercise in the Workbook so you can thoughtfully determine your rat pack, apostles, and tribal leaders.

Once you have a complete list of your Authority Circle, enter them in your contact system (a spreadsheet will do, there's no need to get fancy). I like to keep a notes field to track what we've done together and where we are in the relationship. If your system isn't automated, get in the habit of taking a quick look at your list status at least weekly, so you keep yourself accountable to keep growing those relationships.

Congratulations! You now know who you want to start enlisting to help move your revolution along faster—and farther—than you ever will alone. Believe this: having a clear set of targets is more than half this battle.

What you want to do next is start pollinating your ideas within your Authority Circle. What do I mean by pollinating? In nature, pollinators—bees and hummingbirds—take pollen from one plant to another to fertilize them. But every bee doesn't pollinate every plant. They are quite selective.

Think of your ideas as the pollen. Like bees, you want to carry the pollen only to those most likely to be receptive—a.k.a. your Authority Circle. That's why resonance is so critical here; people who you resonate with are much more likely to be willing pollinators, carrying your ideas back to their tribes.

Enlisting Your Rat Pack

Enlisting your rat pack isn't difficult—these are your friends after all—but you do have to ask. When working on this book, I reached out to every member of my rat pack and asked for help. Depending on their strong suits, I asked for different things, but you better believe I asked everyone for title feedback, cover design choice, and help to spread the word on my launch.

At one point, I apologized to a friend for a flurry of emails requesting quick feedback, and she wrote, "Don't even! I'm just so glad that I can reciprocate at all for all the amazing advice/ insight you have given me over the years." Trust me; she's given me plenty of incredible help during the same time frame. We have invested in each other for literally decades, and now we both reap the rewards from that.

Rat packs are the most straightforward kind of ties to sustain since they feed us both. And since most of us value and maintain a small group of tight-knit relationships, we naturally work at staying in touch and truly connected.

Just don't overlook their importance when you're working at pollinating your ideas and your authority out to the world. They may have precisely the right contacts or the perfect idea of reaching a pivotal tribal leader (I've been known to wake up with a specific idea and email it to a pal).

Get in the regular habit of swapping ideas and challenges and encouraging your rat pack when you know they're frustrated or wavering at the edge of something big. Don't be afraid to add structure around this if it suits you both—just do whatever it takes to stay truly connected.

Enlisting Your Apostles

It's not like we point to a few people in our circle, tell them to jump on our cause, and they cede their life over to our ideas. Apostles are volunteers. They decide what about you and your ideas they genuinely believe, and, over time, they share their version with their people. They might not have classic tribes of their own at all—just a few friends in the business or a few hundred social media connections—but a real desire to share your wisdom. Or, they might also be tribal leaders, which means they have the power to leverage, sometimes on a very grand scale.

When I worked with "Glenda" during the launch of her second book, I encouraged her to make a master list of all the people who might be instrumental in getting some early buzz. She kept resisting and finally fessed up as to why: she didn't want to face possible rejection by the peers that had touted her first book. She feared they wouldn't support this book since it was heavily targeted to a client demographic they were all interested in attracting. She was ready to tell absolutely no one about her new book.

I convinced her just to make the list even if she decided never to contact a single one. Her final list topped out at 174 people (not too shabby, eh?), but here's what's more interesting. We went through the list together, looking for potential apostles, and found fourteen likely candidates that she'd be willing to contact.

Every single one responded positively.

So we designed a plan to involve them in the launch that respected their time, treating them like the busy, highly visible people they were. Of those fourteen, eight proved to be pivotal, leading to a handful of high-profile media interviews, two speeches, and some large, group sales. Two did nothing, which was ironic since one of them offered way more than Glenda ever would ask. Four were helpful (and very much appreciated) but without real impact on the overall launch.

The value of reaching out to those fourteen can't be understated, not even because of their delivered outcomes. Knowing that she was so valued by people she respected gave Glenda a boost of confidence, and she eventually made her way through all 174 names. Did every door open to her? Nope. But the momentum those first fourteen delivered made all the difference to making her launch successful. Apostles are the bomb.

Enlisting Tribal Leaders

Like Glenda, we usually work our way up to enlisting tribal leaders. They are the gatekeepers to their kingdom; they have a direct channel to an audience that will likely resonate with your ideas. The best tribal leaders are hyper-focused on bringing value to their people. They don't let just anyone onto their platform, but they are also practical, they may be willing to throw the dice on a relative unknown IF you can show them how your interests align. Think: editors of an industry publication, hosts of a pivotal show, or a blogger who has built a tribe of engaged followers ripe for your point of view.

They might be idea mavens. These are the thinkers and writers who influence your ideal audience. You resonate with their ideas, their style, and their voice. They may be firmly established or just getting started—but if you're resonating, they are probably good relationships to develop.

And not infrequently, they are peers, as Glenda discovered to her delight. These are the others in your space—perhaps including clients—who are making an impact on the people you want to reach. You can see how your worldviews overlap, even if you sometimes "compete."

In the last chapter, I asked you to pick one way to publish your content—article, podcast, column, etc. Let's say you've been writing articles for your own audience and have a pretty good feel for what will grab them. You're a decent writer, and feel you're ready for greater exposure of your work to a larger audience. And on Your Authority Circle Worksheet, you identified three possible tribal leaders whose audience interests dovetail with your expertise:

> The editor of a niche industry digital outlet.

> The host of a podcast in your niche.

> A blogger with a 50,000-member email list.

What's the best way to get yourself in front of them?

> **Go direct.** You might be surprised at how often this works, provided you're not mindlessly pitching to anyone with a pulse. This action might look like a direct email appeal—which has worked for countless publications big and small when it's carefully crafted and targeted (and you've first tracked down and followed any published submission guidelines).

Ask for an introduction or referral. We get more than a few of these on our podcast when a former guest suggests we talk to someone they know because it feels like a fit. You might check LinkedIn to see how you're connected to whomever you want to reach and ask for an intro. Your best chances for a yes are when every party gets something of value: new ideas targeted for this audience, the satisfaction from doing a favor for your sponsor, and of course, exposure for you.

Offer a get-acquainted favor. Maybe you would love to be on your hero's podcast, but you don't quite have the "celebrity" of their typical guests. Play the long game and invite your star onto *your* podcast or interview them for an article you're writing. Most will say yes, and you'll produce a mutual asset that you can both use repeatedly. But perhaps even better, you've created the chance for a relationship to spark. Keep organically nurturing that spark over time, and you may well become allies.

Become *their* apostle. We're not talking about a superfan who gushes over every tweet, but a thoughtful supporter who shares their best bits and adds value to them for your audience. It's hard for your target to ignore the smart people in their audience who consistently add value to online conversations.

Make introductions. Please use this one very cautiously because what you think is a great introduction may just add to their workload—and not in a good way. Offering to broker an introduction to a contact after your target has mentioned their desire to meet them is an excellent idea. Introducing them to your stockbroker is not.

How To Pitch

As the recipient of countless baaaaaad pitches, let me suggest some ideas, so yours doesn't wind up in the trash folder. The golden rule to pitching yourself is always this: invest in a bit of legwork so you'll know what they'll value—and pitch only that. Luckily, if you're smart about it, it's a small investment of your time with potentially big payoffs.

Read a good assortment of their stuff, and if it's a podcast, listen to a few episodes. Take notes on what they like and their point of view. Has your subject matter been covered before? What can you bring to the party that is fresh and new? Make it easy for them by suggesting up to three one-sentence topic ideas that you believe will be mutually beneficial.

Study how and when they use guest articles or have guests on their show. I once pitched a man for a previously all-woman guest podcast, and you can bet I brought that up in my opening. While it was a no, she gave me a thoughtful response, and we found another way to collaborate.

If you haven't done much podcast guesting, start with smaller audience podcasts where you have a high-value match. They'll be happy for the opportunity to delight their audience (and feed that content beast), you'll get some valuable experience, and you'll both add to your network.

It can sometimes help to demonstrate your audience power, especially if you see value in cross-pollinating. Maybe you share all your interviews with your email list of 1,000 CTOs—that could be catnip to the right tribal leader.

Your actual pitch can be pretty straightforward, with a four (short) paragraph format:

> In your opening, connect to their blog/site/podcast— mention an episode or an insider's thing that shows you did your homework.

> Segue to how your expertise can help their audience—and suggest one to three possible topics.

> Offer no more than three links, including a guest episode if you're pitching podcasts, so they can check you out if they're intrigued.

> Close with a sincere thank you.

And before you hit SEND, check one more time that you've spelled their name correctly. Nothing is more irritating than feeling like you couldn't be bothered to make it *correctly* personal.

If you don't hear from them, respectfully follow up (you'd be surprised at how often a little nudge results in a yes). It is that simple to craft and close a winning pitch. You don't have to be a creative genius or even a dazzling writer. You just have to care enough to pitch only when you can demonstrate the genuine value you'd provide their audience.

One simple rule that works when it comes to spreading your authority: give generously and give often.

And no, you don't have to be a martyr. Adam Grant, author of *Give and Take: Why Helping Others Drives Our Success,* describes "otherish" giving as the most successful of all reciprocity styles in relationships. Unlike selfless givers, otherish givers are smart and strategic about their giving. They've learned to successfully navigate a world with matchers (*I do you a favor and I expect one in return*) and takers so that others don't take advantage of their giving nature.

Like "Max," who is at his happiest doing favors for people he likes. He has a column on a prestigious industry website that took him a few years to negotiate. Yet when someone in an allied field approached him for an introduction to his editor, Max went one better. After ensuring she was the real deal, he didn't just introduce her, he used his influence to pitch her as a columnist (she got the deal). Later, when a similar request came up, he declined to help when it was clear the requestor had a history of being a taker.

Enlisting your best people—your rat pack, apostles, and tribal leaders—is essential to growing your authority. And it's challenging to do from up on the mountaintop; you've got to interact with real people, show up, and give generously. The good news, especially for introverts? We're talking about a relatively small number of people who can tilt your influence—an average of twenty to 150 souls.

You can forget convincing masses of people here—that's what your publishing is for. Enlisting is a one-to-one exercise best performed in small batches with as much smart generosity, humanity, and authenticity as you can muster. How quickly and sustainably your authority grows depends on it.

Enlisting your Authority Circle takeaways:

- Unlike publishing, enlisting your Authority Circle is more of a one-to-one exercise. You're not blasting out content, but listening carefully and connecting, human-to-human.

- Your first circle is your rat pack—those roughly in your business space where you have a high level of resonance.

- Your second circle is your apostles—the people preaching your message not because they get some advantage, but because they *believe.*

- Your third circle is tribal leaders—people leading tribes of their own who resonate with your ideas.

- What counts most in building your Authority Circle is resonance because people with whom you resonate are much more likely to carry your ideas back to their tribes.

- Identifying a clear Authority Circle is essential to growing your authority exponentially—only then can you get in the regular habit of providing value and searching for collaboration opportunities.

- Rat packs are the easiest kind of ties to sustain since most of us are wired to value and maintain a small group of tight-knit relationships.

- Tribal leaders are the gatekeepers to their kingdom with a direct channel to an audience that will likely resonate with your ideas.

- The golden rule to pitching yourself to tribal leaders is always this: invest in a bit of legwork so you'll know exactly what they'll value—and pitch only that.

- When it comes to spreading your authority, give generously and give often.

CHAPTER 9

MASTER THE GENTLE ART OF PERSUASION SO YOU'LL NEVER HAVE TO SELL AGAIN

"Persuasion is achieved by the speaker's personal character when the speech is so spoken as to make us think him credible. We believe good men more fully and more readily than others: this is true generally whatever the question is, and absolutely true where exact certainty is impossible and opinions are divided." —Aristotle

Many freelancers and experts do not enjoy selling their services, which I've always found a bit curious. What's more interesting than listening to an ideal client describe their situation and figuring out how to help them?

Sales conversations are some of the most fun I have during my workday, even if it becomes clear I'm not the right match. It's a chance to listen to a new challenge and apply my thinking to it, offering options that I believe will get them where they want to go.

If you don't like selling, maybe you're thinking of another version of sales, like the fast-talking used car sales guy we all love to hate—who wants to be that guy? And thank goodness, since the hard sell doesn't work when you're selling expertise. ("Hey there, can I interest you in a spiffy new website? I've got a killer deal that's good today only . . .")

Buyers of expertise want to be gently persuaded by your point of view, your track record, and how you demonstrably care about them and their challenges.

They don't want you to sell them on something—in fact, your ideal clients will wind up selling YOU on working together when you've consistently demonstrated your value and fit. The beauty part? If you're following The Authority Code, your point of view and track record are already out there, working on your behalf.

In a sales conversation, if you've been pre-vetted by your clients as an expert or an authority—you don't have to sell. Ever. You can focus on listening to your client and showing that you care deeply about them and their challenges. If you've done the prep work and laid the right cookie crumbs, they arrive to that call predisposed to work with you.

Let's be absolutely clear: I'm not saying you can or should waltz into a sales conversation and never demonstrate your expertise. Instead, I'm saying that by publishing and proving your expertise in advance, the meeting becomes 100 percent about helping your prospect: understanding their situation, their challenges, and the outcomes they seek.

You have the freedom to focus on listening vs. deciding what you're going to say next. You're fully present and attuned to the nuances of the meeting (which is especially helpful if you've got a room full of people). You'll ask penetrating questions that, by themselves, prove your authority. And that's when sales calls become fun. There is a flow to them that almost feels magical. Seriously.

Think of this as the gentle art of persuasion. In a sales meeting, your influence is very subtle—it's in how you listen, ask questions, and synthesize their challenges and opportunities. Working in a tight niche tends to hone your persuasion skills to a very fine point—once you've seen a specific situation many times, you know what to do when things go sideways.

All of this is to encourage you to embrace persuasion to build your authority business. Don't let a fear of or distaste for sales keep you from reaching your full potential as an authority and a business owner. *You can do this.*

The Power Of Establishing Gates

Before we talk about how to master the sales conversation, let's first discuss setting up your sales gate(s). A gate is what you use to decide which prospective clients gain entry to your various levels of attention. And the first level of personal attention is often an informational call or sales conversation. What attributes, challenges, or desired outcomes must you see to entertain a sales conversation?

When you're just getting started, you'll probably let more people through the gate; that's to be expected. You're learning the attributes of your ideal client while you build your business. You'll probably take more meetings (and even new clients) at this stage. But as you get busier and more experienced, you'll tend to be more discerning about the people you spend time meeting.

When I first met "Brendan," he met with any potential client who expressed the remotest interest in his style of Agile consulting. Not surprisingly, his hit rate was near zero since he hadn't differentiated himself from the hordes of Agile consultants. Frustrated, he committed to making the shift to building authority, and as he moved through each step, he got more and more selective about how he invested his time.

His publishing—which had morphed to a particular niche within the Agile space—was attracting a more focused audience who began reaching out for project help. Eventually, Brendan became less interested in project work and moved toward retainer advisory relationships.

Today, he works only on retainer, has a handful of sales conversations every year, and has a waiting list. Because he has highly targeted who he wants to work with and the outcomes they value, his hit rate is now over 90 percent. And yes, he has a very healthy mid-six-figure business.

Sales Conversations

Authorities and authorities-in-the-making don't pitch; we have sales conversations. And if your goal is to engage clients (we'll talk about buyers later in this chapter), you'll want to have as many sales conversations with your ideal prospects as you need to reach your revenue goals.

If your revenue target is $150,000 this year and your average project is $30,000, you need five new clients. If you usually close half your sales conversations, you need ten calls on average, or about a call a month, to make your number. Of course, if you can increase your average project or your hit rate, you can make more money or just work less.

So, how effective are you at sales conversations right now? One sign to look for is how often your ideal prospects convert to clients after a sales meeting. If you're a recognized expert in your niche meeting with a motivated client, your hit rate will probably be 80 percent or more—it might even be well over 90 percent like Brendan's when you align your positioning with your publishing.

Does that mean you're a miserable failure if your numbers are lower? Of course not! It likely means one of two things: your sales gate may be TOO open (you're meeting with unqualified prospects), or you've got room for improvement in your sales conversations. Thankfully, both are fixable.

Adjusting your sales gate may be as simple as going back to the YOUR CLIENT AVATAR exercise and comparing your ideal client to the people you've been meeting with who have not hired you.

What do your nonstarters have in common with each other? Maybe they are just wrapping their arms around the problems you solve and aren't ready for a deep commitment to change. Are there signs before you have a sales conversation that this is the case—and are there changes you want to make to your Client Avatar to reflect this?

Or you might take the long view that even though they are not ready for you yet, talking to them now is a good investment for when they become ready.

Here's the thing: as you identify your ideal clients, pick a niche and start publishing and enlisting the like-minded, your sales conversation opportunities will multiply. You'll keep adjusting the gate as you move forward; there will be people you're excited to speak with today who might not make it through the gate a year from now.

Mastering The Sales Conversation

Mastering your next sales conversation will be easier than you think because you've worked hard to know who you want to work with and what outcomes you'll reach together. This clarity means you're not pitching this client to work with you; you are interviewing them to see if you'll be a fit. Let me repeat that because this one thing might change how you sell your expertise for the rest of your life.

A sales conversation is never a pitch. It's your chance to interview your potential client to decide whether they're a fit.

When you decide your sales conversations are interviews, your hit rate increases (and you adjust those sales gates to admit only better fits). All of a sudden, that anxious feeling, "How will I convince them I'm the one for this work?" slides away. Any adversarial tendencies such as, "How can I get them to pay me enough to make this worthwhile?" just don't get stoked. Now, both parties are meeting to see if and how they might work together.

In most sales conversations with a motivated client, you'll be searching for the answer to three questions.

Why this? You want to understand why they want to do whatever it is they're asking you to provide. If they want you to develop a new website, why? What's it supposed to do? How will they know when that goal is met? Your sales conversation is your chance to not only dig down for their motivations, but if your work is value-priceable, this is how you'll uncover the value behind the work you propose.

The value is never the thing itself; the value is what your client perceives the thing will bring them, e.g., developing a new website means new customers, which means increased revenue (bonus points when you help them put a number on this).

Why now? This question will help you tease out how committed and ready your clients are to move forward. Sometimes the "why now" is because they have budget to be used before year-end. While not exactly scintillating as a why, that might be enough to get your project off the ground, especially if it's extra-pair-of-hands work.

But if your work requires large-scale disruption, you will want much more commitment than having some budget available. Keep probing to find some substantial clues that they are a likely candidate for your best outcomes.

Why me? This idea can feel like a crazy, vulnerable one to dig into, but bear with me for a sec. You might ask why they wouldn't do this work in-house or why they wouldn't use a firm they've worked with before. Or why not someone with slightly different expertise—"Why are you thinking you want a marketing expert when we're talking media relations?" By exploring their thinking, you're naming the elephant in the room.

Maybe they didn't think about this, or maybe that's their real Plan A, and you're an option for Plan B. By bringing up sometimes thorny questions in the sales meeting, your prospective client can see that:

1. This isn't your first rodeo.

2. You have the confidence to discuss anything that impacts the work.

3. You care about them and their outcomes, i.e., they can trust you.

Focusing on those three questions in the flow of the sale conversation changes the dynamics between you and your prospects. You align with each other instead of positioning yourselves in opposite corners.

If they don't feel like the right fit, you can bow out gracefully now, and you're not wasting your valuable time writing a proposal. And if you're not the right fit for the client, they are much more likely to say so after you've demonstrated what open, candid communication looks like (also saving you from writing a doomed proposal).

Sometimes, consulting in a sales conversation leads your client to decide NOT to proceed with hiring you now. Those can be wins in disguise because whether they solve the problem themselves or kick the can further down the road, you've demonstrated what it feels like to work with you. If it's positive, they'll remember next time they need your brand of expertise.

Any time you can give value like that in a sales conversation, you're investing in the relationship, and it will likely bear fruit in the future. Maybe not this year, maybe not even for that project or that company, but in some way with the people who were in that room. Or maybe it's just good karma for the next sales call.

It's the way experts and authorities conduct themselves with their ideal clients.

Products And Productized Services

I've worked with more than a few freelancers who couldn't wait to start adding products (books and courses) or productized services (assessments and service-in-a-day offerings) to their product/service ladder because they'd be perfectly happy if they never had to conduct a sales conversation again.

If that's you, selling products or productized services where your buyer just clicks "BUY THIS" might be the perfect fit with how you want to work and optimally monetize your expertise. It's a great way to leverage your talents and ratchet up your income while reducing the time you spend with actual clients. Just remember, since your price points are lower, you've got to reach considerably more clients and buyers compared to a pure consulting model.

Most freelancers and consultants transition to products and productized services over months and sometimes even years, depending on how quickly the new mix takes hold with their audience. That means you'll want to design your website for the mix you're currently selling while positioning yourself for where you want to go. And that's easier than it sounds.

Persuading From Your Website

Your website is the hub of your authority. It's where you ultimately want to direct your ideal clients (your goal will usually be to get them to sign up for your email list so you can keep them in your circle). You want to design the site to do the heavy lifting of persuading your ideal clients and buyers to pull the trigger.

To do that, you'll need to make five decisions to optimally design your site to build authority and persuade your ideal audience to give you a serious look.

Decision #1: Who is the site for? You've identified your ideal client and buyer in Chapter 3, and now is where you go all in. You're dialing into how they think and speak, their top challenges (or dreams) where you (and your options) are the perfect solution. You might even design a few "Heck, yeah!" headlines—the kind where your ideal client is saying "Heck, yeah!" to each one.

Decision #2: What visitor experience will most closely convey what it's like to work with you or buy your stuff? You've got a style and a voice, and your website is the place to bring it on. Even if you are the very top authority in your field, your site needs to offer a thoughtful experience designed to mimic what it's like to be in a room with you. This is your chance to wow your ideal people and repel the bad fits.

Decision #3: What's your main message? You've chosen your main message in Chapter 2, and now you want to find multiple ways to carry it out on your site. I like developing sound bites—single sentences that pack a punch (check out your BUILD YOUR POINT OF VIEW exercise in Chapter 7—it will likely be sprinkled with ideas you can turn into sound bites). No matter what page your visitors hit, they should feel like it ties to your main message and leads your revolution.

Decision #4: What's the one thing you want your visitors to do? Authority sites most often prioritize lead generation, so they are all about incenting visitors to part with their email addresses. If that's you, you want to test various combinations of lead offers and calls to action until you find the right combination to grow your list.

Decision #5: How do you want to demonstrate your authority to enlist your ideal people? Most people think an authority site had better be content-rich with exceptional levels of deep thinking. And while that may be the case for some, it is not required for all. You are building a particular brand of authority that aligns with the services and products you're selling. If you've written ten books and are the world's leading authority on quantum physics, then yes, you better have some serious depth of content.

But most experts on the authority path need just one or two ways to demonstrate their brand of knowledge, especially in the early years of their business: a blog, a podcast, a video series, a research report, an e-book. What you care about most is that your medium matches your genius zone and your ideal client's preferences while leading them on the path to buying whatever you're selling.

Your website is premium real estate. You must design it so that it performs as your chief persuasion and selling hub—it's not about being "pretty" but about being your workhorse, 24/7, 365 days a year.

Once you've made your five decisions, you can go over your current site in minute detail, questioning every page, every line of copy, every image to ensure they are aligning to tell the story you most want to tell.

Testimonials

One of the most critical elements on any authority website is your testimonials. Your people are spending big bucks on hiring you or buying your stuff, and they want to know what your ideal clients and buyers think about you. Whether you keep your testimonials all in one place, separate them by their specific sales pages or sprinkle them throughout the site, they are the social proof that persuades without selling—in other words, pure gold.

The best testimonials are from ideal clients and buyers, in their words and with their photos and real names (you can up your game with video testimonials, but they don't consistently outperform static images since they take longer to absorb). This truth often challenges coaches due to the confidential nature of their work and client sensitivity. But don't just roll over—try seeking permission to use photo-less testimonials with something like "Disney Production Vice President" so your web visitors can get a feel for your clients.

Testimonials are easiest when they're a natural flow of your work—when as you finish project work or reach a time-bound mile marker, you ask for feedback. It's as simple as this:

> Hey Joe,
>
> I'm thrilled we were able to (insert outcome of your work together or current mile marker). I've enjoyed working with you and your team and so appreciate (insert the mutual good feelings that came out of this work).
>
> You are exactly my ideal client (buyer, student, member), and I'd love it if you would consider writing a testimonial to help other people in your shoes see how we worked together

from your perspective. I'd welcome a few sentences for my website along with permission to use your photo, if that's OK.

All my best,

Sam

If you don't have a stack of testimonials already lying around, you can do something very similar. Just send some of your best clients and buyers an email that you're updating your website and would love to include their testimonials. You may have to follow up once or twice (more than that, and they're probably not going to give you one, so cease and desist) since these requests tend to fall to the bottom of their inbox.

Email Welcome Sequence

A well-thought-out automated email sequence might be the best sales/persuasion investment you ever make.

While a complete discussion of email welcome sequences is a book in itself, let's at least agree that the right one will pay dividends over and over again. For authority purposes, your best bet will be a nurture sequence, where your goal is to introduce your ideal clients and buyers to the world you're creating for them—and keep them connected to you as they become immersed.

Most authority business models don't rely on a first-time website visitor making a purchase. Instead, they know they must enlist their people and take them on a journey. The goal is not to make an immediate sale but to gently persuade them that this new world is where they want to live (or send them running for the exits if they aren't your ideal audience).

Some might never buy anything from you—and that's perfectly OK. You are the generous authority, giving ideas and insights away to many and selling services and products to a subset of this group.

Generous authority Jill Konrath has spent most of her consulting and speaking career giving away valuable advice to tens of thousands of salespeople while earning her money from a very narrow slice of paying clients. You won't see her employing a hard sell—or even a soft sell; it's all about giving generously to further her mission of accelerating sales.

That's persuasion vs. selling. Persuasion is focused on your audience but tied to your ultimate vision for the world and business you're creating. Finding the right balance for your business and revenue model just might mean you'll never have to sell again.

Mastering the gentle art of persuasion (so you'll never have to sell again) takeaways:

- Buyers of expertise want to be gently persuaded by your point of view, your track record, and how you demonstrably care about them and their challenges.

- When you've been pre-vetted by your prospective clients as an expert or an authority, you don't have to sell. Instead, you're interviewing them to see if they are a good fit.

- Don't let a distaste for sales keep you from reaching your full potential as an authority and a business owner.

- You'll define gates to decide which prospective clients gain entry to your various levels of attention, and you can expand or contract these as you grow your business.

- Authorities and authorities-in-the-making don't pitch; we have sales conversations.

- In sales conversations with motivated clients, you'll be searching for the answer to three questions: why this, why now, and why me?

- Your website is the hub of your authority which means you want to design the site to do the heavy lifting of persuading your ideal clients and buyers.

- Make five key decisions to demonstrate authority on your website and align every image, piece of copy, and flow of the site to those decisions.

- The best testimonials are from ideal clients and buyers, in their words, with their photos and real names.

- Invest in a nurturing welcome email sequence where your goal is to introduce and connect your ideal clients and buyers to the world you're creating for them.

CHAPTER 10

TAKE YOUR AUTHORITY
OUT FOR A SPIN

"While we may be tempted to hustle to get our authority, to somehow prove that we are right, we are actually giving up authority when you do that because in our culture, the signals that come with authority are not the same as the signals that come from the desperate chase of proving you're right." —Seth Godin on **The Business of Authority**

Congratulations! If you've done the work in each of these chapters, you're ready to take your authority out for a spin!

By now, you know that building your authority is not a "desperate chase of proving you're right." Hopefully, words like "hustle" and "hack" make you cringe—because they always sound rather desperate, and that's the opposite of the authority I want for you and your business.

But you do have to *act* on all this work you've completed. Keeping your expertise to yourself or a too-small group of believers is a waste of your potential. You can begin small—starting to publish in your niche or pivoting your content to better fit your new positioning—and then speed up as you gather momentum.

Or you can move full speed ahead with your new direction, reworking whatever isn't aligning with your positioning. That could mean major shifts in how you market yourself (website, social media, communications), as well as how you monetize and sell your expertise (your service/product pricing/mix; how and where you publish; who you spend time enlisting).

There is no universal right way to proceed other than first making sure that you've got your basic financial needs covered so you're not wondering where your next buck is coming from.

This is where you take a deep, deep breath. You've done the heavy lifting of getting clear on how to position yourself, your business, and your expertise. You've decided how best to monetize that positioning so you can work in your genius zone and build a six-figure-plus business. And, you've decided how to publish your expertise and enlist your people so you can leverage and sell your authority far easier than you do today.

EXERCISE 12: YOUR AUTHORITY ACTION PLAN

Now that you've got your authority elements in place, it's time to make—and execute—your action plan to roll all this out. Because until you take it out of the theoretical and into your day-to-day world, it won't be working for you.

Here's where you need to pull out your Workbook, which will guide you through getting all the elements in one place so you can build your custom action plan.

Once you've drafted your action plan, use this checklist to ensure you've reviewed all your client-/buyer-facing materials:

Website

- Copy

    - Does it appeal to your target and align with your new positioning?

    - Is your point of view fully expressed?

    - Are your calls to action clear and compelling (downloads, joining email list, etc.)?

    - Does the voice you're using fit how you speak (generally, first person works better than third)?

    - Do your content choices align with your new direction, or do they need a pivot for the future?

- Images

    - Do the shots (or video) of you convey the right balance of authority and approachability?

    - If you're using stock photos or footage, do they look thoughtfully curated to match your message?

- Testimonials

    - Are they from your ideal clients and buyers; will your target audience relate to them?

    - Does their content point out your best outcomes?

    - Are you using their names, photos, and titles in a way that will appeal to your targets?

Social Media

- Profiles

    - Does your headline position you as an expert or authority in your space?

    - Does it reflect the right balance of business/social for that platform?

    - Is your photo the same modern, on-brand shot you use across all your (business) social profiles?

- Content

    - Do you need to shift what you're posting based on your publishing plans, including your lanes of content?

    - Are you consistently demonstrating your point of view?

    - Does your byline position you as an expert or authority in your space?

- Engagement

  - Do you need to change how you engage or who you engage with based on your new authority positioning?

  - Do your targeted media leaders use this site, and if so, are you following and interacting with them?

  - Are you consistently demonstrating your point of view?

Email Marketing

- Email template: Does the look and feel fit with your brand of authority?

- Welcome sequence

  - Is it designed for your ideal clients and buyers?

  - How will you connect with them— will you ask questions, offer chances to talk, meet, etc.?

  - Have you designed a path for them to get to know, use, and eventually buy your content?

  - Is the technology working for you, or do you need tech help to take advantage of key features?

- List marketing

    - How will you regularly offer demonstrated value to your list?

    - How will you write your emails to encourage feedback, a golden source to better communicate your ideas?

Marketing Collateral

- What documents beyond your website are you using to tell your world about you and your business?

- Where are you maintaining a presence beyond social media, such as:

    - Industry websites

    - Any site where you search for contract help or employees

    - Slack channels with clients, prospects, and/or peers

    - Publications (digital or otherwise) where you maintain a contributor profile

    - One-off sites where you might mix business and personal, such as Amazon reviews, Quora comments, etc.

Quashing Your Limiting Beliefs

Before you can truly step into becoming the authority you were meant to be, you've got to recognize and tamp down (or better yet, stamp out) any beliefs that put arbitrary limits on what you can do and achieve.

We all have limiting beliefs. When I ran track in high school, I compared myself to my friend Jenny—she was faster, smoother, and, well, incredible. She won every race with ease, and while we trained together, I didn't take it all that seriously since she was so much better than me, until I lucked into qualifying for a regional 400-meter race (the girl who won the spot ahead of me had dropped out).

After the starting gun, I realized I was up against some serious competitors and was so not in their league. Coming in dead last was embarrassing (it still makes me squirm to think about it). I was ready to slink away, but Jenny bet me that I could take at least five seconds off my time (i.e., not finish last) if I got serious about it. Once we made that bet—I think it was $1—there's no way I would lose. I trained like a fiend and eventually shaved eight seconds off my time.

My limiting belief? That I was not a runner. I let the fact that I didn't start as the best—or even close to the best—dictate my thinking, which translated directly into my actions. And yes, I kept running after high school (until I discovered biking).

Maybe you've experienced some of the limiting beliefs I've heard when it comes to authority:

I can't make money doing that.

Why would they hire me? I don't have . . . (a master's degree, twenty years of experience, perfect health, etc.).

I'm not good at . . . (selling, writing, speaking).

I'm too . . . (young, old, fat, thin, bald, tattooed) to do that.

I don't deserve a place at that table.

But if I do this new thing, how can I ever explain it to . . . (my peers, mother, father, spouse, old boss, mentor)?

What if this new thing fails and I have to get a job again— what will I tell my family?

Can you see the common thread in all those? Yep, it's fear— which, by the way, is perfectly normal. Only the clueless don't stop to think about the downsides of their future moves. When you believe the potential outcome is worth the risk, the key is to act anyway.

Once you know your limiting beliefs, you have the power to change them.

I can make money doing that.

I can learn how to write better.

I (will) deserve a place at the table with my icons.

You just might be surprised at how reframing your self-imposed limits opens up your opportunities to succeed in new ways that suit how you want to work, live, and serve your people.

One last word on this—well, actually two: impostor syndrome. I continue to hear from some fiercely talented people (you would be gob-smacked at how good they are at their craft) who feel like impostors. I'm betting that at some point in your career, maybe even now as you contemplate taking a bigger stage, you could relate.

If you spend time feeling like an impostor, I say *bring it on!* Of course, you feel like an impostor if you're doing work that matters.

As Seth Godin said when we interviewed him on *The Business of Authority*: "You can't certify that you've done this exact thing before and it's guaranteed to work. You can't. So, because you're a good person and an honest person, inside, you feel like a fraud because . . . you're describing a future that isn't here yet. And if you're not feeling like an impostor, I would argue you are not working hard enough."

Mic drop.

A Few Last Thoughts

The road to authority I've described here is simple but not always easy. It requires you to position, monetize, and sell your expertise in a powerfully unique way that reflects your sweet spot—the overlap of your talents, passions, and a segment of the market thrilled to align with you.

I encourage you to do the work in this book to find that sweet spot so you can carve out a business that speaks to you, your audience, and the world you want to create. That allows you to live the life you crave in every way—financially, physically, emotionally, and spiritually.

And if you don't hit nirvana the first time out (or your definition of nirvana is changing)? Never underestimate the power you have to position or reposition yourself, your expertise, and your business at any time. You can add, subtract, or double down on your products and services. You can increase your prices regularly as your demand grows or repackage your offerings at lower price points so you can reach more people. You can even start building a new Authority Circle.

Becoming and remaining an authority requires adopting an authority mindset—channeling generosity and abundance, endless curiosity; listening more than you speak; courage, confidence, and grace under pressure—all while consistently bringing the world one step closer to your vision.

If you want more support to continue on your road to authority, visit my website at *www.rochellemoulton.com/*, where you'll find plenty of free resources as well as opportunities to engage in AuthorityNation (my group coaching program).

Thank you for spending this chunk of your time with me. I hope that exploring how to turn your expertise into a happy, profitable, sustainable authority business reaps dividends for you, your fans, and your circle for many years to come.

Be unforgettable,

Rochelle

ACKNOWLEDGMENTS

I'd like to thank the people most impacted by my obsession with this book:

> My husband, Harvey, who did all the grocery shopping, served me a beautiful breakfast (on a tray!) every morning and walked Jackson when I couldn't break away from a writing spree. He patiently listened while I read portions out loud and unfailingly believed in me and this book. How did I get so lucky?
>
> The ever-loyal Jackson who not only sat at—or on—my feet through it all, but let me know when it was time to take a break (or give him a treat).
>
> The band of pals who kept encouraging me (and even made a pot of soup to keep me going): Rebecca, Ginny, Donna, and Jonathan.

My deepest gratitude to my extended family who always believed: Nana, Grampa, Dad, Judy, Scotty, Julie, Laurie, Aunt Joan, and every single one of my Gamache uncles—Phil, Dick, Bob, and Marty.

Thank you so much to the amazing people who've helped me shape the ideas in this book and improve my craft—it really does take a village:

Adam Davidson, Andrea Barry, Angela Jones, Ant Pugh, Beatrice Felix, Bert Keeter, Bill Ferdinand, Blair Enns, Bob Greene, Bob Lalasz, Bob Lopes, Bryan Moll, Calvin Lyons, Carl Allegretti, Carleen MacKay, Candace Chapman, Carol Henriques, Charles Green, Christina Okubo, Corey Bearak, Dan Coffey, Dave Mangot, David C. Baker, David Maister, David White, Don MacDougall, Donna Grummich, Doug Johnson, Ed Rosenbaum, Emily Omier, Gary Pines, George Stocker, Harold Kain, Ken Fox, Jill Konrath, Joanna Conti, Joe Jacobi, Jonathan Stark, Josette Goldberg, Julie Kohler, K. C. Victor, Kathy Blanton, Kathy Layne, Karen Richards, Katie Speth, Kelli Cruz, Lisa Riley, Manville Smith, Marcia Inch, Marco Pelusi, Mark Bryan, Mark Treichel, Martha Watt, Martha Yount, Matt Day, Michael Hais, Michael Kay, Michael Zipursky, Morley Winograd, Neil Schaffer, Pat Stoller, Patience Reich, Paul Klein, Peter Block, Ramona Russell, Rebecca Wear Robinson, Sabrina King, Saqib Rasool, Sarah Lewis, Seth Godin, Thomas Hripko, and Wayne Pollock.

The moment I spotted editor Lia Ottaviano, I knew we must work together and she graciously agreed to take me on. Lia, your guidance and thoughtful edits have given me renewed confidence in my writing. Thank you for honing my craft with your special brand of magic.

Xavier Comas took my book idea and brought it to life—seeing his cover designs thrilled me to my toes and I thank you.

Heather Pendley confirmed that proofreading—even after extensive copy editing—is an essential art in producing a readable book. Thank you for making me clearer and sharper than when left to my own devices.

Thank you to Sara Franklin who took my raw exercises and morphed them into a stunning Workbook and to Darryl Suiter who makes all my digital systems sing.

And to those who contributed directly to spreading the word on this book, a huge, heartfelt thank you:

> Ajit Shaw, Alastair McDermott, Anila Patel, Ben Berry, Benedicte Rae, Bob Greene, Bob Lalasz, Brandon Curran, Chris Catteau, Chris Do, Christina Okubo, Daniel Taylor, Dave Mangot, Denise Calhoun, Donna Myrow, Doug Heikkinin, Ellen Gardner, Erin Austin, George Stocker, Geraldine Carter, Jackie Brown, Jacob Lett, Jason Urmacher, Joanna Conti, Joe Jacobi, Jonathan Stark, José Martinez, Karina Schultheis, Kathrin Bussman, Leann Regalla, Mark Taylor, Matt Mullenix, Michael Kitces, Michael Ryan, Michelle Garrett, Mike Bird, N. Chloe Nwangwu, Nick Vivion, Oak Agsornsin Muayman, Paul Klein, Rebecca Wear Robinson, Rev. Dr. Louise-Diana, Samuel Ng, Scott Maxwell, Sherryl Maxwell, and Stephen Bishop.

And finally, I'm beyond grateful for the thoughtful and generous big idea authors and authorities who inspired me in writing this book—I urge you to read their works and apply their thinking to your authority business:

Adam Davidson, Adam Grant, Al Reis, Anders Ericsson, Andrew Sobel, Angela Duckworth, April Dunford, Betty Sue Flowers, Caroline Myss, Chandler Bolt, Charles Green, Chris Anderson, Daniel Pink, David C. Baker, David Maister, Elizabeth Gilbert, Greg McKeown, JL Collins, James Clear, Jen Sincero, Jill Konrath, Jonah Berger, Jonathan Stark, Julia Cameron, Kevin Kelly, Marie Kondo, Mark Bryan, Marty Neumeier, Michael Gerber, Michael Hais, Michael Kay, Michael Port, Morley Winograd, Nancy Friday, Peter Block, Paul Jarvis, Priya Parker, Robin Fisher Roffer, Seth Godin, Steven Pressfield, Suze Orman, and Vicki Robin.

ABOUT THE AUTHOR

Rochelle Moulton turns consultants and big thinkers into authorities. She led introverted brainiacs at two powerhouse consulting firms and turned around the failing consulting arm of a Fortune 500 company. She built three professional firms from scratch—and sold one to Arthur Andersen. She co-hosts *The Business of Authority* and has been featured in *The Wall Street Journal* as a forward thinker in the consulting space. *www. rochellemoulton.com*